Paper Birds That Fly

Paper Birds That Fly

Norman Schmidt

Sterling Publishing Co., Inc.   New York
A Sterling/Tamos Book

A Sterling / Tamos Book
© 1996 Norman Schmidt

Sterling Publishing Company, Inc.
387 Park Avenue South, New York, NY 10016

TAMOS Books Inc.
300 Wales Avenue, Winnipeg, MB, Canada R2M 2S9

10   9   8   7   6   5   4   3   2   1

Distributed in Canada by Sterling Publishing Co., Inc.
c/o Canadian Manda Group, 1 Atlantic Avenue, Suite 105
Toronto, Ontario, Canada M6K 3E7
Distributed in Great Britain and Europe by Cassell PLC
Wellington House, 125 Strand, London WC2R 0BB, England
Distributed in Australia by Capricorn Link (Australia) Pty
Ltd.
P.O. Box 6651, Baulkham Hills,
Business Centre, NSW 2153, Australia

Design   Norman Schmidt
Photography   Jerry Grajewski & Walter Kaiser,
                          Custom Images
Printed in Hong Kong

CANADIAN CATALOGING IN PUBLICATION DATA

Schmidt, Norman Jacob, 1947-

    Paper birds that fly

    "A Sterling/Tamos book."
    Includes index.
    ISBN 1-895569-01-X

1. Birds – Models.   2. Birds – Flight.   3. Paper works.
I. Title.

TT870.S35 1996   745.592   C95-920249-8

LIBRARY OF CONGRESS
CATALOGING IN PUBLICATION DATA

Schmidt, Norman.
    Paper birds that fly / Norman Schmidt.
          p.   cm.
    "A Sterling/Tamos book."
    Includes index.
    Summary: Describes the use of the different parts of a bird's
wings and tail and the maneuverability of its feathers. Includes
patterns and instructions for fifteen paper birds.
    ISBN 1-895569-01-X
    1. Paper works — Juvenile literature. 2. Birds in art — Juvenile
literature. 3. Birds — Flight — Juvenile literature. [1. Paper
work. 2. Handicraft. 3. Birds in art. 4. Birds — Flight.]
I. Title.
TT870.S326   1996
745.592 — dc20
                                              95-49194
                                                 CIP
ISBN 1-895569-01-X Trade   AC
ISBN 1-895569-11-7 Paper

Contents

The Flight of Birds

Many people are bird watchers. Seeing birds flit and soar easily about the sky has always held a special fascination for earthbound creatures. We watch and admire and are inspired to become airborne ourselves. Bird flight motivated the human pioneering spirit, which led to experiments with various kinds of flying machines. But no one understood how birds remained aloft. Consequently, in the early days, there were many unsuccessful attempts at human flight.

Failures occurred because people were sidetracked by the most obvious thing that birds do — wing flapping. People saw birds sitting at rest with their wings folded neatly at their sides, and suddenly, with a furious flapping motion, take off and become airborne. Wing flapping was thought to hold the answer and this is what many of the early experimenters concentrated on. They tried to imitate a bird's flapping wings, and that is why they failed. Flapping flight is more than the up and down motion of wings. It is actually a complex operation, and a bird's wing is a complicated piece of machinery, not easily copied.

Two kinds of flight

The flight of birds is divided into two main kinds — gliding flight and flapping flight. All birds, with the exception of hummingbirds, utilize both kinds at one time or another during the course of each flight. (There are two other kinds of flight — hovering flight that is a particular kind of flapping flight done by many birds, especially humming birds, and diving flight that is a particular kind of gliding flight used especially by some birds of prey.) In the two main kinds, birds use their wings differently at different times to achieve the desired result. A bird's wing seems to have a two-part function. People were slow to realize this because the wing's rapid motion made its operation difficult to observe. Not until the invention of stop-action photography could accurate observations be made.

A bird's wing can be compared to a human arm consisting of several parts — shoulder, upper arm, elbow, forearm, wrist, and hand. Each of these parts of a bird's wing is covered with different kinds of feathers. When a bird flaps its wings up and down the various parts, with their various feathers, perform different functions. Had early experimenters realized this, human flight might have occurred much earlier. It was only when experimentation turned from flapping to gliding flight that real progress was made in understanding how lift is produced. All the flapping in the world would never actually get a bird airborne had the wings not first had the capabilities of gliding flight. And lift-production is where one must begin, even today, to understand the flight of birds.

But before the specifics of bird flight can be examined, it is necessary to understand how air interacts with solid objects. Aerodynamics is a good place to begin. Comparing aircraft and birds can show us how their various parts contribute to flight.

People long ago were inspired by the flight of birds. These drawings from ancient Egypt show birds in flapping flight and gliding flight. They may have been drawn six thousand years ago, suggesting that people have for a long time noticed different ways that birds fly.

5

The skeleton of a human arm is compared to that of a bird. The bird's hand has many fewer bones.

How Flight is Achieved

Aerodynamics

Air is a gas, and like water it is fluid or flowing. Solid objects can be immersed in it. The entire earth is surrounded by a layer of it. Air presses against everything from every side. All objects are enveloped by it and interact with it. Yet we cannot see directly how air behaves because it is invisible. So how can we form any opinion about it? We can observe its effects on objects in it. Air, like all fluids, can be still or in motion. When air moves we call it wind. We have seen wind rustling leaves and bending trees, or even uprooting them. We can feel it on our faces when we run fast.

When a moving fluid and a solid object interact there are certain natural forces at work. Fluids flow, swirl, and eddy around solid objects. You may have seen how a rock in a running brook causes the water to swirl. A solid object has the same affect on air. Aerodynamics is the study of how moving air behaves around solid objects. Its study began with a Swiss scientist, Daniel Bernoulli, who lived in the 1700s. He noticed that as the speed of a fluid past a solid object increases, the pressure that it exerts outward decreases. He published his findings in 1738 in a scientific paper called *Hydrodynamica*. Today we call his discovery Bernoulli's Principle.

Flight depends on the fact that the natural forces of moving air, along with the force of gravity, can be controlled consistently so they work together harmoniously. In all, there are four forces that must be dealt with in flight. They are gravity, drag, lift, and thrust.

Gravity

Gravity gives objects weight and makes them earthbound. All objects on earth are acted upon by this force which is provided by the earth itself. Every object has a center of gravity. It is that point at which all the weight of the object appears to be concentrated and the point at which the object balances. In order for flight to take place, this is where the object must be lifted. Gravity must be overcome by the lifting force created by the wings.

Drag

All objects are made up of small particles, called molecules. The molecules of a fluid are farther apart than those of solid objects. They can be moved apart even farther. Just as when we swim we push water molecules aside, so too when we move in air, we push air molecules aside. But the molecules also resist our movement. They don't move out of the way freely. They must be pushed, and the faster you wish to move

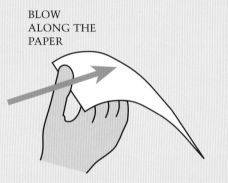

BLOW ALONG THE PAPER

Holding one short end of half a sheet of paper between thumb and forefinger, let the paper droop over your hand. Then blow over your thumb and along the paper. Which way does the paper move? If done correctly the paper should rise because the moving air exerts less pressure downward than the air beneath the paper does upward. This is Bernoulli's Principle.

Why does the paper droop over your hand? It droops because the force of gravity pulls the unsupported end downward.

them, the more they resist, so the more you must push. This is the reason we can feel the wind when we run. The faster we run, the more the air resists. That is why running into the wind on a windy day can be hard work and why a belly-flop in water can hurt. When a fluid moves very fast, as air does in a hurricane or water when squirting from a hose, the molecules have the capability of knocking over solid objects. The resisting force of air molecules is very important to flight. It is called drag.

Lift

Birds and airplanes remain airborne in exactly the same ways, abiding by the same laws of nature. It is the shape of their wings as they move through the air that affects air molecules in a particular way, causing the molecules to create a lifting force. And this lifting force must be directly over the object's center of gravity. That is why the wings of birds and airplanes are positioned at their centers of gravity.

Lift-production depends on air pressure. Air pressure gives air its force. The layer of air that surrounds the earth presses against everything with varying degrees of pressure from place to place, depending on the weather. Also, pressure is greatest at sea level, gradually decreasing with altitude until the air peters out and outer space begins. High pressure means that the molecules are more closely packed together. Low pressure means that they are farther apart. The ability of air to have high or low pressure is vital to its ability to create a lifting force. Except for wind, we are ordinarily unaware of air pressure. Pressure is another way of describing drag.

When a bird or an airplane flies, the wings slice the air into two layers, one above and one below the wings. Both layers are made up of the same number of molecules. But if the wing has a curved upper surface, the molecules moving across the top surface have farther to travel than the ones underneath, if they are to maintain their position in relation to the rest of the air molecules. Therefore the molecules on top become spaced farther apart and increase their speed so that when they reach the back edge of the wing, they again match their position with the lower molecules.

In accordance with Bernoulli's Principle, the faster moving and more widely spaced upper molecules exert less pressure downward than the slower moving and more closely spaced lower molecules do upward. There is a pressure difference above and beneath the wing. The lower pressure above the wings creates suction, much like a vacuum cleaner. The higher pressure beneath the wings pushes upward. Acting together, these forces bouy up the bird or plane. Because the wing has to move air molecules aside, all lift-production also creates an accompanying amount of drag.

The difference in pressure above and below the wings, and the amount of lift produced, can be increased if the front edge of the wings is raised

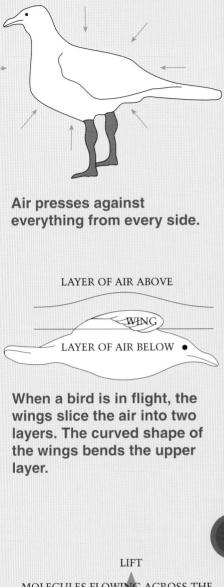

Air presses against everything from every side.

When a bird is in flight, the wings slice the air into two layers. The curved shape of the wings bends the upper layer.

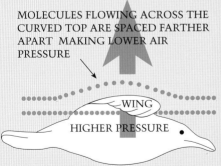

The lift created by the wings is dependent on a difference in air pressure above and below them.

7

slightly, allowing air molecules to strike the slanted lower surface, giving an added upward push.

This upward angling of a wing is called the angle of attack. The greater the angle of attack, the greater the lifting force becomes. But the drag also increases. As the angle is increased, more and more molecules strike the bottom of the wing resulting in more and more drag until the force is backward instead of upward.

When a particular angle is reached, air flowing across the top of the wings no longer flows smoothly but breaks into eddies and becomes turbulent. At this point lift production stops. The wing becomes stalled. This occurs at an angle of about 15 degrees. This increased drag is useful for braking when landing.

The creation of lift, therefore, is entirely dependent on how the flow of air about the wings is controlled. Any curved airflow-controlling surface is also known as an airfoil. In aircraft, the curved shape of the airfoil is designed into the ribbed structure underneath the wing covering. In a bird, the shapes of the wing feathers give shape to the airfoil. Each feather has a curved hollow center structure, called a quill, that is flexible but strong. On each side of the quill are the wind-catching vanes. Birds can freely move their wings, adjusting their shape, and changing the angle of attack. But airplane wings are more or less fixed. Birds therefore have a great deal more control of the flow of air than most aircraft.

The strength of the lifting force is directly dependent on the speed with which air moves across the wings. The faster a bird or plane flies, the greater the lift. From a dead stop, it takes a lot of energy to attain lift-off speed. That is why airplanes need long runways, with engines running at full throttle, to get airborne. Some birds, like geese and flamingos, have to run for a long distance on the water before they can take off. And some water birds, like loons, cannot take off from land, where their legs are not strong enough to give them lift-off speed. But small perching birds that don't weigh very much in relation to the lifting force of their wings, can attain lift-off speed almost as soon as they begin to move forward.

Thrust

This is the force that moves a bird or airplane forward, acting against the resisting force of the air. In gliding flight, the lifting force of the wings prevents the force of gravity from pulling the bird or plane straight downward. Instead, gravity pulls the bird or plane forward and downward, while the wings bouy up the weight. Thus gravity creates thrust. The bird or plane is pulled by gravity along an invisible layer of air in a gentle downward glide, just as a sled is pulled by gravity down a snowy hill. Birds and aircraft (unless they are gliders) can, of course, also take off and climb into the air by utilizing their wings (birds) and propellers (planes). The flapping motion of a bird's wings generates added thrust and added forward momentum, as does the spinning propeller of an airplane.

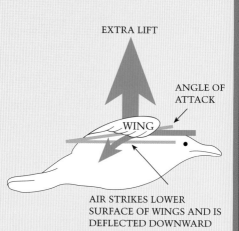

The lift created by the wings is increased if the front of the wings is raised slightly, creating an angle of attack. This allows air to strike the lower surface which provides an added upward force.

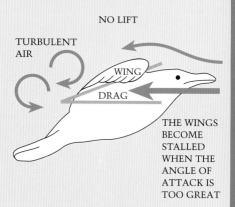

Lift stops if the front of the wings is raised too much because the air flowing over the top breaks into eddies. Then the air striking the bottom surface creates a backward force (drag) instead of upward. The wings are stalled.

8

But how does a propeller work? An airplane's propeller is actually a smaller airfoil attached to a central hub about which it spins. And the principle of its operation is identical to that of a wing. As an airplane's propeller spins, this small "wing" slices the air into two layers with different pressure, creating lift. However, the "wing" is moving in a vertical space instead of a horizontal one. Therefore its "lift" is not upward, as with the airplane's wings, but forward. This force drives the airplane forward through the air.

There are, therefore, two types of thrust: one provided by gravity in gliding flight, and the other provided by the spinning motion of a propeller or the up and down motion of a bird's wings in flapping flight. Both types are used by aircraft and birds at various times as demanded by changing flight situations.

When an airplane or a bird flies, the four forces are at work harmoniously, acting in two pairs — the force of lift overcomes the force of gravity, and the force of thrust overcomes the resisting force of drag. In level flight these forces equal each other, and are in perfect balance.

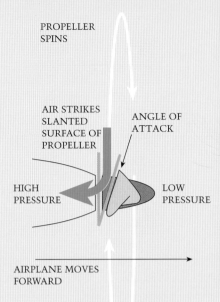

PROPELLER SPINS

AIR STRIKES SLANTED SURFACE OF PROPELLER

ANGLE OF ATTACK

HIGH PRESSURE

LOW PRESSURE

AIRPLANE MOVES FORWARD

The blades of a propeller are small "wings." The "lifting" force they create as they spin about is directed forward instead of upward. This creates a backward thrust driving the airplane forward.

9

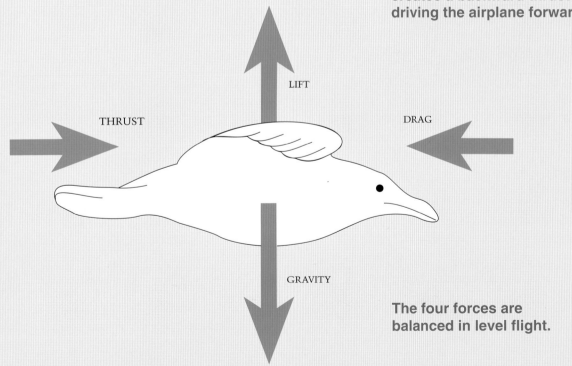

LIFT

THRUST

DRAG

GRAVITY

The four forces are balanced in level flight.

How Bird Wings Work

At one time people thought that birds flying through the air were engaged in an activity much like rowing a boat across water, with the downstroke being "active" and giving a forward push, and the upstroke being a "neutral" return stroke. Little was understood about the interaction of the four forces of gravity, lift, drag, and thrust. Nothing was understood about the complex actions of the various parts of a bird's wings to create the forces necessary for upward and forward flight.

The wings of a bird are divided into inner and outer parts. The inner sections nearest the body pivot about the shoulder joint. The outer sections move separately, pivoting about the wrist joint. A bird's elbows allow the wings to fold. It is the inner parts that are the airfoils that provide the lifting force required to keep the bird in the air. They are the equivalent of an airplane's wings. The feathers of the inner sections are the secondary feathers. They have the smooth curved tops necessary for creating a pressure difference above and beneath the wings as they slice through the air. Adding to the curvature are the small covert feathers.

The outer "hand" parts are the bird's propellers. They have the long flight feathers, referred to as the primary feathers. Throughout each wing beat, sweeping up and down, the primary feathers are constantly changing their shape, adjusting to the resultant changes in air pressure.

Flapping flight

On the down beat, the primary feathers twist and bend to stand almost at right angles to the wing itself. This adjustment is due to the shape of each of the primary feathers. The vanes on the forward facing edge of each feather are much narrower than the rearward facing ones. When air strikes the feathers, the force is greater on the wider vanes than on the narrower ones. This difference of forces on the forward and rearward vanes twists the feathers. On the down beat of the wings, the greater force on the rear vanes twists each feather upward, bending the quills until the outer wing section assumes the correct angle to act as a propeller by directing airflow backward.

The primary feathers are not fastened solidly to the bone like teeth, but are attached by a flexible cartilage that allows them freedom for the required twisting motion.

The outer parts of the wings and the primary feathers are wonderfully adaptable to a variety of flight situations. For a sudden takeoff, and when a bird is flying fast, each wing beat is strong, creating a lot of twisting motion. Then the entire length of each primary feather twists and is utilized to make a propelling force. In leisurely flight, when the wing beats are light, only the outer tips of each feather twist to provide propulsion. The greater the twisting motion, the greater the propelling force (backward flow of air) becomes.

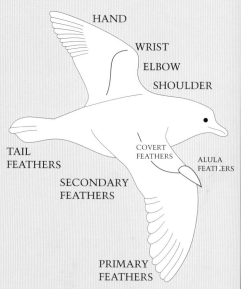

A gull in flight, showing the parts of the wings and the bird's main feathers.

A feather, showing its parts and its flexibility.

However, the wings do not merely move up and down with each beat. On the down beat the wings also move forward, and on the up beat they also move backward. The amount of forward and backward motion can be adjusted by the bird as required. When a bird takes off, for example, the wings beat very rapidly and the motion is as much forward and backward as it is up and down. In leisurely flight the motion is slower and more nearly only up and down. In some birds, pigeons and grouse for example, the forward motion is so great that the the primary feathers strike together like hand clapping, creating a slapping sound during a quick take-off. In each complete flapping cycle, the path traced by each wing is downward and forward on the downstroke, and upward and backward on the upstroke, making for a sloping figure-eight path.

As the down beat begins, the bird holds the entire wing fully extended. A strong down stroke causes the air pressure to press together the primary feathers, allowing no air to slip between the feathers along the entire length. This maximizes the propelling force created by the wings for takeoff and rapid flight as air is deflected backward. At the end of the downward stroke, the bird flexes its wrists as the upward part of the cycle begins. This partly folds back the outer sections. At the same time the primary feathers are slightly separated, like fingers on a human hand, by the flexing motion and the resulting change in air pressure. As they separate they also twist and open up like venetian blinds and air can slip between them. In small birds this decreases the drag, making for a quick up beat in which no propelling force is created. In larger birds, each feather becomes a separate airfoil, creating lift as well as exerting a forward momentum. As the wrists flex, the outer parts of the wings bend in an upward angle and rise first as the entire wing sweeps upward. At the end of the upward sweep, the outer parts of the wings are given a sudden burst of power, flapping outward, resuming their position for the next down beat. The down beat is always stronger and takes more time to complete than the up beat.

Simultaneously, while the outer tips of the wings are acting as propellers driving the bird forward, the inner parts of the wings are held at a more or less constant angle of attack to provide the lifting force required to bouy up the weight of the bird, even though the dihedral angle (upward slant) is constantly changing with the up and down motion. However, the bird can alter the angle of attack to maintain a steady lifting force as required at any time as the forward speed of the bird changes. It can also vary the degree of flapping motion.

Flight maneuverability

The dihedral angle of bird and airplane wings is their upward slanting away from the body. Obviously in flapping flight this changes constantly for birds. They can easily control the amount of dihedral angle during flight as required. But in most aircraft the dihedral angle is fixed. The greater this angle , the more stable the flight, and the less vulnerable to

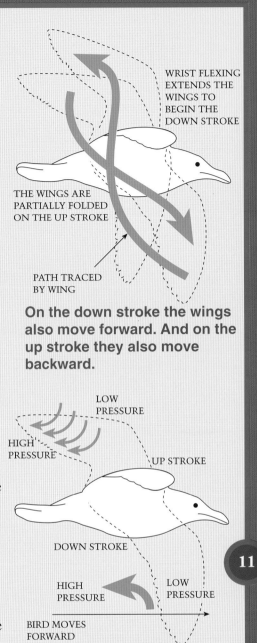

WRIST FLEXING EXTENDS THE WINGS TO BEGIN THE DOWN STROKE

THE WINGS ARE PARTIALLY FOLDED ON THE UP STROKE

PATH TRACED BY WING

On the down stroke the wings also move forward. And on the up stroke they also move backward.

LOW PRESSURE

HIGH PRESSURE

UP STROKE

DOWN STROKE

HIGH PRESSURE

LOW PRESSURE

BIRD MOVES FORWARD

On the down stroke air strikes the lower surfaces of the primary feathers and is deflected backward. On the up stroke the feathers separate and air slips between them to reduce drag. The feathers twist in such a manner that air is still deflected backward by each feather individually. This is a bird's propeller.

upset because of gusty wind. However, the greater the angle the less lift there is. A large dihedral angle makes for less maneuverable flight.

Fighter planes, for example, that must be able to zoom about the sky, have little or no dihedral angle built in. Some even have the opposite, a downward slanting away from the body, called anhedral. This makes for very unstable flight, but is great for maneuverability. Planes used for cropdusting have a large dihedral angle for stability. Birds, on the other hand, with wings that can move freely, can utilize the maneuverability of an anhedral angle of their wings if they need to quickly change the direction of their flight. Some birds alight with their wings in a near vertical position, raising them slowly to decrease the lifting force as they come in for landing.

A bird's tail also plays an important part in controlling flight. And the control is much more subtle than an airplane's tail. Most airplane tails have a horizontal surface and a vertical surface. They control the wing's angle of attack and keep the body, or fuselage, as it is called, pointing into the airflow. But a bird's tail has a number of more or less straight feathers. On each side of the tail, the feathers have similar vanes. This symmetry allows them to evenly control the airflow on each side of the bird. The feathers can be spread out or folded together, like a Chinese fan. They can be tilted up or down, and rotated left or right. This flexibility gives the bird its delicate control. In fact, it is by fanning or tilting the tail that the bird can maintain a constant wing angle of attack throughout each wing beat. Or the angle of attack can be changed as required for different speeds, especially in landing. Fanned wide, the tail is used as an air brake to control speed. It also keeps the bird's body pointing into the airflow, and is used to compensate for gusty conditions. Without its tail, a bird would have great difficulty flying.

During takeoff a bird needs all the lifting force it can muster so that a force powerful enough to get airborne is created at the earliest possible moment while the forward speed is still relatively slow. This is also true for airplanes. The wings of some aircraft have flaps at the front and back edges that bend down, making the distance across the curved surface longer and increasing the lifting force during slow flight. Similarly, birds have small ancillary feathers, called the alula feathers (see p 10), attached to the wrists. During slow flight these are extended to increase the wing's lifting force. They are also extended in a quick takeoff.

Gliding flight

Once a bird is airborne it can resort to gliding flight at any time by stopping its flapping motion and keeping the wings extended at some suitable dihedral angle. In gliding flight the entire length of the extended wings become lift-producing. Both the inner sections, that are always lift-producing, and the outer sections, that are usually the propellers, now produce lift. Once in gliding mode, the bird immediately begins to

The upward slanting of the wings away from the body is called the dihedral angle. It provides stability in flight.

The tail can be rotated, fanned out, and raised or lowered to create extra drag. This helps to provide balance and maintain the wings' angle of attack by tilting the body up or down. It can also slow down speed as well as prevent upset in gusty conditions.

descend very gradually as gravity pulls it downward and forward. The same is true for aircraft if the engine is throttled back or shut off. At any time a bird can resume flapping, or a plane can turn on its engine, and gain height again.

Birds, like airplanes, combine powered and gliding flight. Gliding is always used for landing. Some aircraft, however, have no engines and no propellers. They are pure gliders. For takeoff a glider is towed by another airplane that does have an engine and propeller. Once at a suitable height, a few thousand feet in the air, the glider releases from the towplane and begins gliding flight. Some birds, such as albatrosses, are almost pure gliders. They cannot take off unassisted. Spreading their wings, they take off as they are bobbed up by the wave action of water. From the ground, they can only take off from a clifftop.

Soaring flight

Interestingly, the air in the sky above us is not still, but in constant motion. This gives us our weather. When the sun shines, its rays heat up the ground. This heat is then radiated to the air immediately above it, which warms up. Warmer air is always lighter than cooler air. Being lighter than the surrounding air, the warmed air begins to rise, as bubbles rise in a kettle of water heating on the stove. Once there are enough "bubbles" they combine to form a column of rising air, called a thermal. During a sunny day there are many such columns forming across the countryside. They can rise to great heights, often many thousands of feet high. In hilly country there is another source of rising air. It is found where surface wind is deflected upward by sharply rising ground or a cliff face. In some parts of the world this source of rising air is always present. It is known as ridge lift.

When a glider — either an aircraft or a bird flying in gliding flight — encounters air that is rising faster than the rate at which gravity is pulling it downward, the plane or bird no longer descends but begins to soar. As long as it can stay in rising air a plane or bird can actually climb and gain height. Gliders can climb to the tops of thermals. This is how they use thermal lift for sustained flight. Circling round and round, they climb in one thermal, then glide in gently descending flight until another thermal is encountered. There they climb again. In this manner they can soar for hours. To utilize ridge lift they fly parallel to the crest of a hill or cliff, staying in the rising air that is being deflected by the ground.

Some birds spend much more time in gliding flight than flapping flight and are known as soaring birds. On a sunny afternoon when ground heating is at its greatest, hawks, eagles, condors, that are the finest land soaring birds, can be seen circling gently in the invisible columns of rising air forming over the fields. Or they skim the crests of hills. Water birds such as gulls, petrels, and albatrosses also soar, either over land or over water. Over water, the smaller gulls and petrels soar on the air being

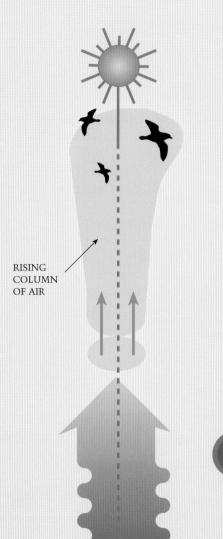

RISING COLUMN OF AIR

13

On a sunny day the earth is warmed by the sun's rays. This heat is radiated into the air which then becomes warmed. The warm air, being lighter, begins to rise forming a thermal in which soaring birds can stay aloft without beating their wings.

deflected upward along the crests of waves. Albatrosses use this kind of ridge lift, but they also utilize the wind gradient as a source of energy in what is known as dynamic soaring. (See p 84.) Albatrosses are the best soaring birds.

What all the soaring birds have in common are wings that are particularily suited to gliding flight. Their wings are large for their body sizes — either very long or very broad. Because of air resistance, such large wings would be difficult to flap for very long periods of time, requiring more power than the muscles of the birds could generate. But these wings are especially well suited to gliding flight. Long narrow wings of birds such as gulls, create much more lift for the accompanying drag. Broad wings are normally poor glider wings. But birds that have broad wings — hawks and eagles — have the ability to separate the primary feathers as they glide, making each feather into a separate lift-producing winglet. This greatly improves the amount of lift for the resulting drag, making the wing more like a long narrow wing.

Many birds, such as sparrow hawks, kingfishers, and especially hummingbirds, can hover. By beating their wings rapidly, fanning their tails up and down, and holding their bodies more vertically, they can maintain their position over the ground as well as overcome the pull of gravity. Hummingbirds can even fly backwards. The sparrow hawk and the kingfisher hover to watch for prey on the ground. When prey is sighted, they raise or partly fold their wings to lessen drag and begin diving flight, pointing sharply towards the ground and rapidly increasing speed as gravity pulls them downward. Many birds swoop down in diving flight at one time or another to catch food or to escape.

Replacing feathers

Feathers, constantly buffeted by wind, wear out. They do not grow continuously, as does hair. At least once each year birds molt. They lose their old feathers to grow new ones. Most birds lose their feathers a few at a time instead of all at once, so they can still fly. Without flight they would starve or be easy prey. However, they are poorer fliers for a time. Other birds, water birds such as ducks, lose all their primary feathers at once. For a time they are flightless. Since they are on the water these birds can both feed and find hiding places. Being flightless does not harm them in any way.

Certainly the flight of a bird through the air is not as simple as rowing a boat on water, as was thought at one time. Ornithologists, people who study birds, have given us much valuable information on the flight of birds. A bird is a masterful and efficiently designed flying machine. A bird's flying action is complex, requiring a harmonious interaction between various forces subtlely controlled by wings and tail. At no time during flight are the wings in "neutral." In gliding flight the entire wing is a lift-producing airfoil. In flapping flight, both the down stroke and the up stroke create both a lifting force (from the inner sections) and a propelling force (from the outer sections).

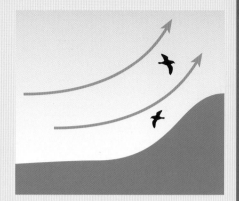

When the wind blows against a hill the air is deflected upward. Birds can skim along the crest, flying back and forth in the rising air and remain airborne without beating their wings.

Wings partly folded, a gull shown in a full swooping dive.

Constructing Paper Birds

The birds in this book can all be made using ordinary 20 or 24 lb bond copier paper measuring 8 ½ in by 11 in (21.6 cm by 27.9 cm). Bond paper is ideally suited to building paper flyers. It is lightweight, easy to cut and fold, and easy to fasten together. It is available in a variety of colors. Since the lift and thrust are limited in a paper flyer, every effort must be made to keep drag at a minimum. Every surface not parallel to the direction of travel (wings, tail, head) adds drag, so the neater and more accurate your construction, the better the bird will fly. Clean and accurate cuts and crisp folds are a top priority. Flapping flight is too complex to duplicate in paper. Therefore the birds in this book are gliders, a method of flight all birds (except hummingbirds) do sometime during the course of every flight.

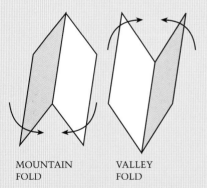

All you need to get started.

Measuring and cutting

Use a sharp pencil to mark the measurements and draw firm, accurate lines. Cut out the pieces with a sharp pair of scissors or a craft knife and a steel-edged ruler. A knife makes a cleaner cut. Where multiple layers are cut, as in the heads of the birds, a knife makes the job easier. For making curves, draw around a coin, jar lid, or pot lid and cut out. When using a knife be sure to work on a suitable cutting surface.

Folding

There are two kinds of folds used in the book. They are mountain folds and valley folds. Always lay paper on a level surface for folding. Folding is easier along a score line. To make a score line, draw a line along a ruler using a sharp pencil so that a slight indentation is made on the paper. Where multiple layers are folded, run your fingers fiirmly back and forth along the fold to make a sharp crease.

MOUNTAIN FOLD   VALLEY FOLD

Mountain and valley folds are actually the same kind of fold. Both are made by folding a flat piece of paper and sharply creasing the fold line. The only difference is that one folds down (mountain fold) and the other folds up (valley fold). They are distinguished only for convenience in giving instructions.

Gluing

A glue stick works best for lightweight paper and is used for all of the birds in this book. The glue not only holds the pieces together, but also, when dry, gives stiffness to the parts. Follow the instructions carefully. Cover the entire contacting surfaces that are to be joined. If there are multiple layers, apply glue to each of the sheets. Glue should be used sparingly, but use enough to hold the parts together. Where multiple layers are being joined you may need to hold the pieces for a few minutes until the glue sets.

Flying Tips

Don't be discouraged if on first flight your paper bird "corkscrews" and crashes. Flying the paper birds is a delicate balancing act. Only when the center of gravity (balance) is correct and the wings and tail are working harmoniously is successful flight achieved. The balance of the bird can be adjusted by changing the weight of the head. You will notice that the number of layers of paper used in constructing the head varies with different birds. Using fewer or more layers is a good way of changing the bird's balance. With each paper bird that you build, aim to improve the construction.

Flying straight

Once you have a well built bird, bend the tips of the tail up slightly to control the glide path and keep the bird from diving toward the ground. But remember, the performance of each paper bird differs. Experimentation is necessary in order to achieve maximum performance. This is part of the fun of flying paper birds.

Careful construction

Folds that are not neat and crisp add unnecessary drag to the bird. This will decrease glide performance. Inaccurate gluing does not help matters. A twisted bird is sure to "corkscrew" badly. The importance of careful folds cannot be overemphasized.

The birds must be symmetrical – one side must be just like the other. On both sides wing and tail sizes, shapes, and thicknesses must be the same. Make sure that all folds are accurate and not sloppy. Also make sure that the wings are not twisted. This will cause the bird to bank sharply.

Make sure that the dihedral (upward slanting of wings and tail) is adjusted correctly. In each design, refer to the last step of construction for suggestions. Sometimes experimentation with different dihedral (or none at all) will be successful. Dihedral provides stability; however, too much dihedral has a destabilizing effect.

LAUNCHING THE BIRDS
Paper birds cannot be thrown hard. To launch, hold the body lightly between thumb and forefinger near the point where the bird balances. Throw with a firm forward motion keeping the bird level, pushing it more than throwing it. With a bit of practice you will discover just how hard each of the birds needs to be thrown in different conditions.

FLY SAFELY
The birds in this book have sharp points so never fly them toward another person. If you fly them outdoors they may go farther than you expect. Be sure they do not go into the street where you will have to retrieve them.

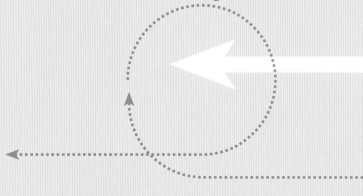

With just the right amount of forward motion, some paper birds can be made to fly a loop.

Coloration

Each bird is shown with a side view and half of the top view in actual size, displaying the wing outline with the primary and secondary feathers, the head, and the tail. Trace these patterns onto your paper birds. Use the suggested color schemes for the birds. Shown is the coloration of the male and female birds in their breeding plumage. However, for the sake of simplicity, only the general feather patterns and color schemes are given. The actual birds are more elaborate in some instances.

Draw the pattern lines using a fine black felt-tipped pen. Colored markers are ideal for filling in. Avoid water-based markers because they wrinkle the paper too much.

It is easier to add color to the birds before they are completely assembled. It is best to color each piece (wings, head, or body) once it has been cut to the correct shape and secured with glue, as required. As the pieces are made, test them for accuracy and fit. Only when all the pieces for one bird are done should the pieces be glued together to form the bird.

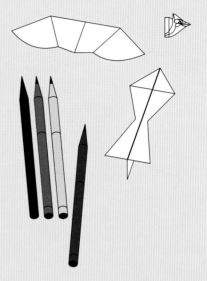

Add color before the birds are assembled.

Hanging Bird Mobiles

Besides flying the paper birds, they can also be hung up for display. Using very fine picture hanging wire works well. First, decide how long of a piece of wire you will need and cut it to length. Then find the bird's center of gravity (the point at which it balances). Do this by holding the bird just as if you are about to throw it. But instead of throwing it, rest the wings on the tip of your thumb and forefinger and move the bird forward and backward a small amount until the balancing point is found. Then on the bird's back, mark the spot. Vertically from the top (the bird's back), use a darning needle to poke a small hole going all the way through the wings and body. Insert the wire, going all the way through. Once through, bend the tip of the wire over, making a small hook. Then fasten the other end to the ceiling, or wherever you wish.

Or you can make a bird mobile. Several birds can be hung from a small twig. Then the entire twig with the birds can be balanced and hung from the ceiling. Or they can be hung from yet another twig, always in such a manner that everything remains balanced. You can make the mobile as complex as you wish.

DARNING NEEDLE

FIND THE BALANCING POINTS

SMALL TWIG

A mobile consisting of a flock of blue jays.

American Goldfinch

It is easy to spot a goldfinch on the wing. Finches demonstrate the relationship between flapping and gliding flight every time they fly. When in leisurely flight, finches use rapid wing beats (about 5 beats per second) to climb for a number of seconds, then partially fold their wings in a gliding dive for a number of seconds. This makes for a roller-coaster-like flight path, flapping up, gliding down, flapping up, gliding down. During the flapping portion of the cycle these birds call out sharply. Finches overhead can often be heard before they are seen.

Goldfinches are truly North American birds, ranging from coast to coast, nesting across the northern part of the continent but staying well below the tree line of the Canadian arctic, and wintering across the southern portion of the United States. Like all finches, goldfinches are seed eaters. Their flying consists mainly in going from one food source to another. In urban areas they are often seen at back yard feeding stations. In the autumn, finches congregate in large flocks in preparation for migration.

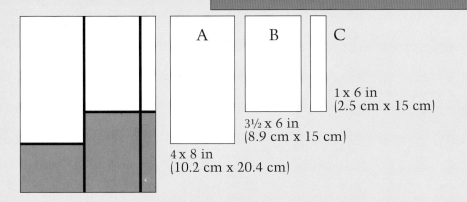

STEP 1   Measure and cut the various pieces from one sheet of bond paper.

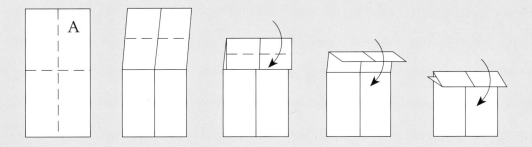

STEP 2   Lay piece A flat in a vertical direction. To make the body, fold in half vertically using a valley fold. Unfold. Fold in half horizontally using a valley fold. Unfold. Valley fold top portion so that top edge meets horizontal crease. Then fold top portion again so that top edge meets horizontal crease. Finally fold over again along original horizontal crease.

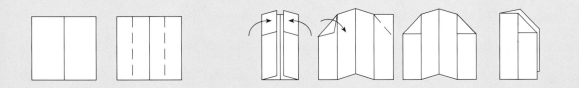

STEP 3   With upper folded part facing to the back, valley fold each side so that outer edges meet center crease, as shown. Unfold. On each side, valley fold diagonally so that top edge meets vertical crease, as shown. Then refold original vertical center crease, as shown.

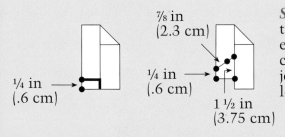

STEP 4   On the left edge, measure from bottom and cut out to the center crease, as shown by heavy line. On the left edge, measure from bottom and mark. Along the center crease, measure from bottom and mark. Draw diagonal line joining the two marks. Measure along drawn line from the left and mark.

19

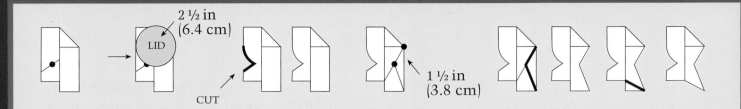

2 ½ in
(6.4 cm)

LID

CUT

1 ½ in
(3.8 cm)

STEP 5   Using the drawn lines as an alignment guide, trace around a jar lid and cut out, as shown by heavy line.

STEP 6   From right-hand corner of diagonal fold, draw a diagonal line to the bottom center crease. From upper point, measure along diagonal line and mark. Draw diagonal line from the mark to the bottom right-hand corner. Cut out, as shown by heavy line. Then cut bottom corner diagonally, as shown.

Leave ½ in (1.3 cm) unglued at the tip

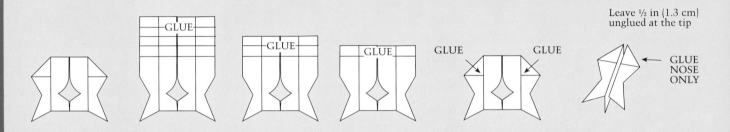

GLUE

GLUE

GLUE

GLUE

GLUE

GLUE
NOSE
ONLY

STEP 7   Unfold body completely. Refold applying glue to all contacting surfaces, as shown. Shape body as shown. Glue nose only, leaving the tip unglued.

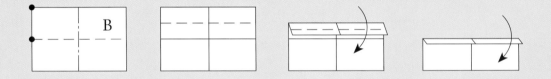

B

STEP 8   Lay piece B horizontally to make the wings. Fold in half vertically, using a mountain fold. Unfold. Fold in half horizontally, using a valley fold. Unfold. Then valley fold so that top edge meets horizontal crease. Fold again so that the new top edge meets the horizontal crease. Refold original horizontal crease.

1 ¼ in →
(3.2 cm)

CUT

GLUE   GLUE

STEP 9   Unfold completely. On each side, measure and cut diagonally, as shown. Refold. Apply glue before refolding original horizontal center crease only. The folded over part is the bottom of the front edge of the wings.

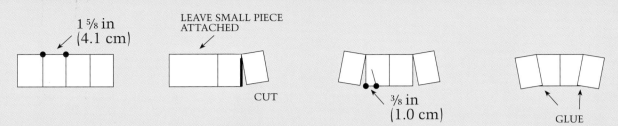

STEP 10 To shape the wings, measure on each side, mark, and draw lines, as shown. Then, on each side, cut from the back edge as shown by heavy lines, leaving a small piece attached at the front edge. From each cut, measure and make a mark on the back edge, as shown. Align outer pieces to the marks. Glue.

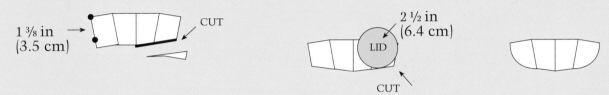

STEP 11 On each side, measure along the outer edge and make marks. Draw lines from bottom center to the marks. Then cut along lines. Trace around a lid and cut out to round the wingtips.

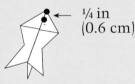

C   1½ in x 1 in
(3.8 cm x 2.5 cm)

NOTE: FOR CORRECT BALANCE, MORE OR FEWER LAYERS MAY BE NEEDED DEPENDING ON THE TYPE OF PAPER AND THE AMOUNT OF GLUE USED

STEP 12 Measure from front of body and mark for wing position. Glue wings in place, as shown.

STEP 13 Using sheet C, measure and cut four small pieces, as shown. On two of the pieces, make a tracing of each side of the goldfinch's head shown on p 22.

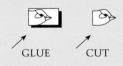

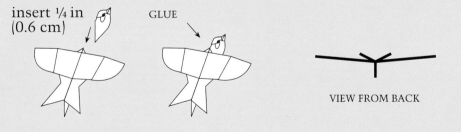

STEP 14 Glue the pieces one on top of the other, having the tracings on the two outer sides, making sure that they are aligned. Then cut out the shape of the head, as shown.

STEP 15 Applying glue, insert the head into the front of the body. Then adjust the dihedral (upward slant of wings), as shown.

American Goldfinch

This paper finch is almost actual size. The goldfinch is about 4 ½ inches (11.5 cm) in length, with a wingspan of 5 in (12.5 cm) when fully extended. The plumage of the male is mainly bright yellow and black, with some white. The primary feathers and tail are black. The head is capped in black. The bill is a darker yellow.

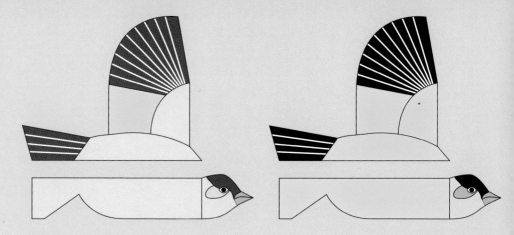

Female coloration   Male coloration

22

BIRD MARKINGS PATTERN

NOTE: ADD PATTERN AND COLOR
AFTER EACH PART IS COMPLETED,
BEFORE FINAL ASSEMBLY

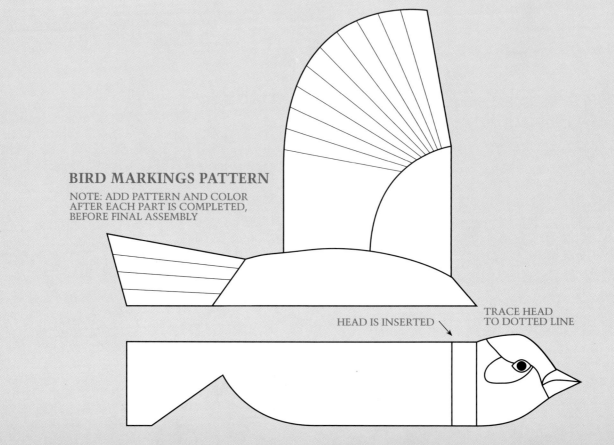

HEAD IS INSERTED

TRACE HEAD
TO DOTTED LINE

Blue Jay

Blue Jays are wanderers, often seen in loose flocks of up to 50 birds. But they are non-migratory in most of their range. They are found in the eastern and mid-western regions of North America. They favor wooded areas. Their wings are broad and somewhat rounded, as are the wings of many birds found in woodlands. They are fast flyers, and except for landing, don't resort to gliding flight very often. Blue Jays sometimes raid the nests of other birds. Therefore they are frequently chased by other smaller birds, especially during nesting season.

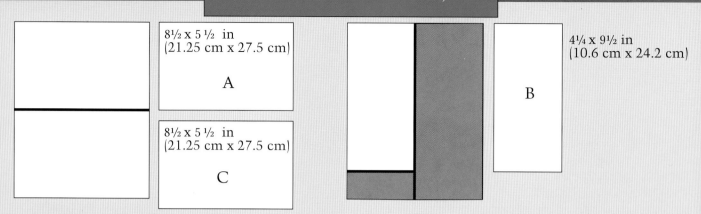

8½ x 5 ½ in
(21.25 cm x 27.5 cm)

A

8½ x 5 ½ in
(21.25 cm x 27.5 cm)

C

4¼ x 9½ in
(10.6 cm x 24.2 cm)

B

STEP 1   Measure and cut the various pieces from two sheets of bond paper.

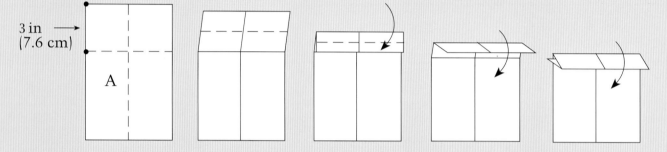

3 in
(7.6 cm)

A

STEP 2   Lay piece A flat in a vertical direction. To make the body, fold in half vertically using a valley fold. Unfold. Measure from top and valley fold, as shown. Unfold. Valley fold top portion so that top edge meets horizontal crease. Then fold top portion again so that top edge meets horizontal crease. Finally, fold over again along original horizontal crease.

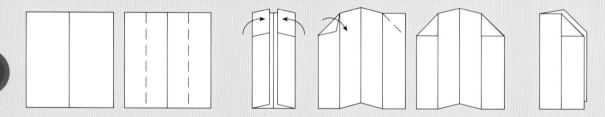

STEP 3   With upper folded part facing to the back, valley fold each side so that outer edges meet center crease, as shown. Unfold. On each side, valley fold diagonally so that top edge meets vertical crease, as shown. Then refold original vertical center crease, as shown.

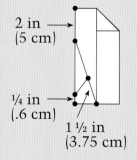

2 in
(5 cm)

¼ in
(.6 cm)

1 ½ in
(3.75 cm)

STEP 4   On the left edge, measure from top and draw diagonal line to bottom center crease. Measure along drawn line from the bottom and mark. On the left edge, measure from bottom and mark. Join the two marks, as shown.

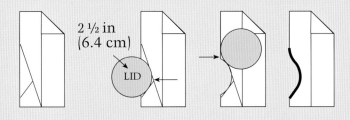 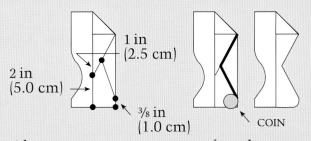

STEP 5   Using the drawn lines as an alignment guide, trace around a jar lid and cut rounded corners, as shown by heavy line.

STEP 6   Along center crease, measure from bottom and mark a point. From right-hand corner of diagonal fold, draw a diagonal line to the point. From point, measure along diagonal line and mark. Along bottom edge, measure from center crease and mark. Draw diagonal line, joining the two marks. Then cut out, as shown by heavy line. Round the bottom right-hand corner by tracing around a coin.

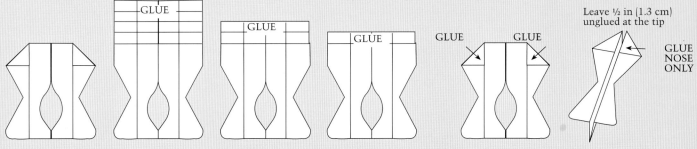

STEP 7   Unfold body completely. Refold applying glue to all contacting surfaces, as shown. Shape body as shown. Glue nose only, leaving the tip unglued.

STEP 8   Lay piece B horizontally to make the wings. Fold in half vertically, using a mountain fold. Unfold. Fold in half horizontally, using a valley fold. Unfold. Then valley fold so that top edge meets center crease. Fold again so that the new top edge meets the center crease. Refold original horizontal center crease.

STEP 9   Unfold completely. On each side, measure and cut diagonally, as shown. Refold. Apply glue before refolding original horizontal center crease only. The folded over part is the bottom of the front edge of the wings.

25

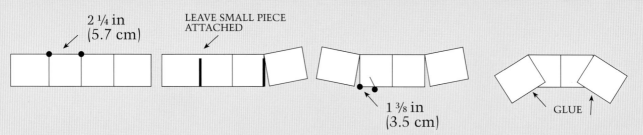

LEAVE SMALL PIECE ATTACHED

1 ⅜ in (3.5 cm)

GLUE

STEP 10   To shape the wings, measure on each side, mark, and draw lines, as shown. Then, on each side, cut from the back edge as shown by heavy lines, leaving a small piece attached at the front edge. From each cut, measure and make a mark on the back edge, as shown. Align outer pieces to the marks. Glue.

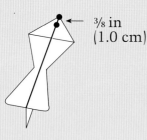

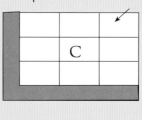

LID

6¼ in (16.0 cm)

¼ in (0.6 cm)

STEP 11   On each side, measure from the back edge along the glued line and make a mark, as shown. Draw line from mark to bottom center. To shape the back edge of the wings, trace around the lid (from a cooking pot) aligned with the mark and the outer wingtip and cut out, as shown by heavy line.

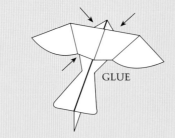

⅜ in (1.0 cm)

GLUE

1¾ in x 2 ½ in (4.5 cm x 6.4 cm)

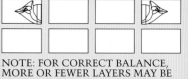

C

NOTE: FOR CORRECT BALANCE, MORE OR FEWER LAYERS MAY BE NEEDED DEPENDING ON THE TYPE OF PAPER AND THE AMOUNT OF GLUE USED

26

STEP 12   Measure from front of body and mark for wing position. Glue wings in place, as shown.

STEP 13   Using sheet C, measure and cut eight small pieces, as shown. On two of the pieces, make a tracing of each side of the blue jay's head, shown on p 27.

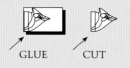

GLUE   CUT

STEP 14   Glue the pieces one on top of the other, having the tracings on the two outer sides, making sure that they are aligned. Then cut out the shape of the head, as shown.

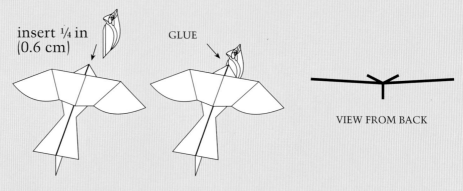

insert ¼ in (0.6 cm)

GLUE

VIEW FROM BACK

STEP 15   Applying glue, insert the head into the front of the body. Then adjust the dihedral (upward slant of wings), as shown.

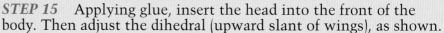

Blue Jay

This paper blue jay is smaller than actual size. The actual blue jay is about 9 inches (23 cm) in length, with a wing span slightly greater when fully extended. Both male and female are similar in coloration. The upper parts are blue with white on the wings and tail. The breast is light gray. Black markings delineate the head. The eyes are black and the bill dark gray. It has a conspicuous crest.

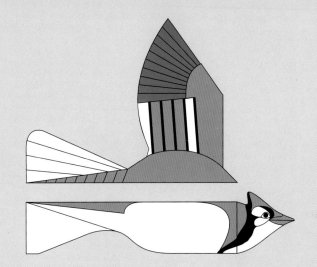

Male and female coloration

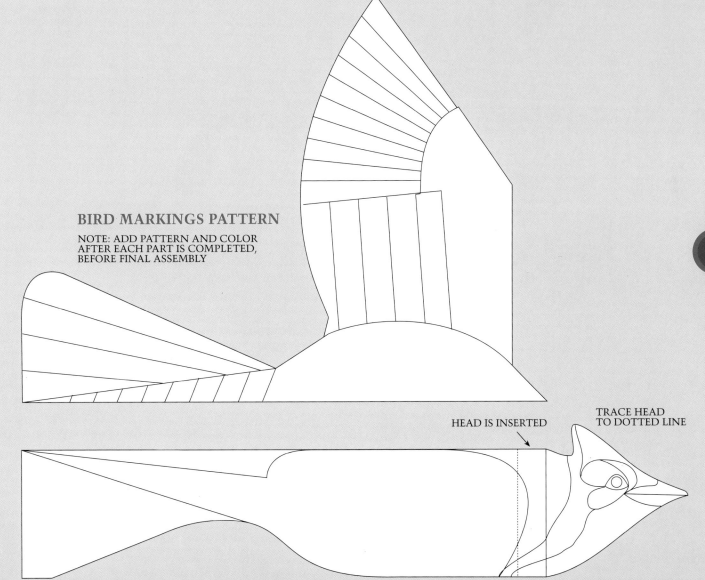

BIRD MARKINGS PATTERN

NOTE: ADD PATTERN AND COLOR
AFTER EACH PART IS COMPLETED,
BEFORE FINAL ASSEMBLY

HEAD IS INSERTED

TRACE HEAD
TO DOTTED LINE

Blue-Footed Booby

Boobies are tropical birds that live along the west coast of South America, migrating north for nesting to the California coastline during the summertime. They are good flyers. Their long wings and light weight allows them to fly at a slow speed. Their wingbeats are stiff, alternately flapping and gliding. To survive, boobies feed entirely on fish by diving to catch them. They are the world's greatest divers. They hunt from the air, searching for schools of fish while cruising slowly over open water about 50 feet from the surface. When prey is sighted, they dive. Because of their light weight, they need to reduce drag as much as possible in order to gain enough speed during their descent to penetrate the water and reach their prey. Boobies do this by completely closing their wings, extending them back and elongating their already streamlined body into a double-ended shape that resembles a torpedo. Therefore they can enter the water at a speed that exceeds 60 mph (100 kph) creating barely a ripple. Having caught their prey completely by surprise, they swim for a short distance beneath the surface before bobbing up and taking off. During migratory flight, they fly at low altitude in single file steadily alternating flapping and gliding.

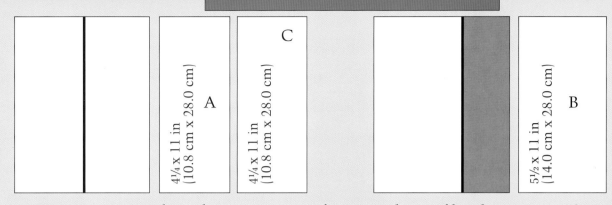

STEP 1 Measure and cut the various pieces from two sheets of bond paper.

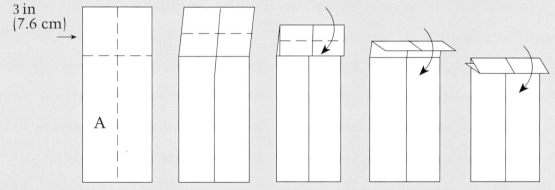

STEP 2 Lay piece A flat in a vertical direction. To make the body, fold in half vertically using a valley fold. Unfold. Measure from top and valley fold, as shown. Unfold. Valley fold top portion so that top edge meets horizontal crease. Then fold top portion again so that top edge meets horizontal crease. Finally, fold over again along original horizontal crease.

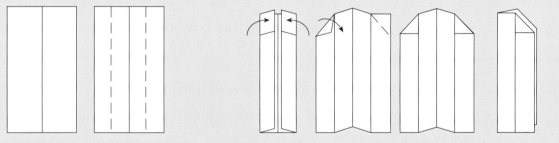

STEP 3 With upper folded part facing to the back, valley fold each side so that outer edges meet center crease, as shown. Unfold. On each side, valley fold diagonally so that top edge meets vertical crease, as shown. Then refold original vertical center crease, as shown.

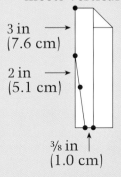

STEP 4 From the top on the left edge and from the bottom center, measure and make marks. Draw a line joining the marks. Measure on the drawn line from the top and mark, as shown.

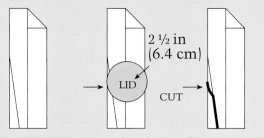

STEP 5 Using the drawn lines as an alignment guide, trace around a jar lid and cut out, as shown by heavy line.

STEP 6 From right-hand corner of diagonal fold, draw a diagonal line to the bottom center crease. From upper point, measure along diagonal line and mark. Measure up from the lower right-hand corner and mark. Draw diagonal line joining the two marks. Then cut out, as shown by heavy line.

2 ½ in (6.4 cm)

LID

CUT

4 in (10.2 cm)

1 in (2.5 cm)

GLUE

GLUE

GLUE

GLUE

GLUE

Leave ½ in (1.3 cm) unglued at the tip

GLUE NOSE ONLY

STEP 7 Unfold body completely. Refold applying glue to all contacting surfaces, as shown. Shape body as shown. Glue nose only, leaving the tip unglued.

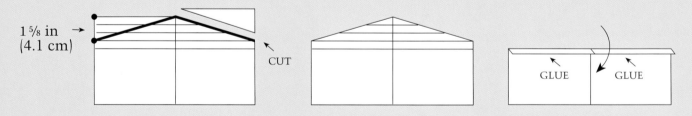

B

2 in (5.1 cm)

STEP 8 Lay piece B horizontally to make the wings. Fold in half vertically, using a mountain fold. Unfold. Measure from top edge and fold horizontally, using a valley fold. Unfold. Then valley fold so that top edge meets horizontal crease. Fold again so that the new top edge meets the horizontal crease. Refold original horizontal crease.

1 ⅝ in (4.1 cm)

CUT

GLUE   GLUE

STEP 9 Unfold completely. On each side, measure and cut diagonally, as shown. Refold. Apply glue before refolding original horizontal center crease only. The folded over part is the bottom of the front edge of the wings.

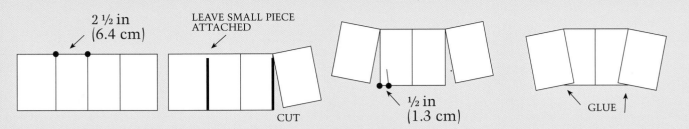

STEP 10   To shape the wings, measure on each side, mark, and draw lines, as shown. Then, on each side, cut from the back edge as shown by heavy lines, leaving a small piece attached at the front edge. From each cut, measure and make a mark on the back edge, as shown. Align outer pieces to the marks. Glue.

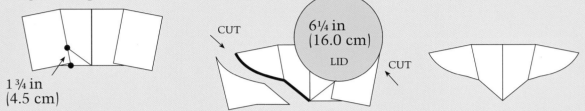

STEP 11   On each side, measure from the back edge along the glued line and make mark. Then draw line from the mark to bottom center. Cut along line and trace around a large lid and cut out to shape the wingtips.

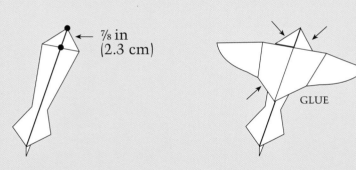

STEP 12   Measure from front of body and mark for wing position. Glue wings in place, as shown.

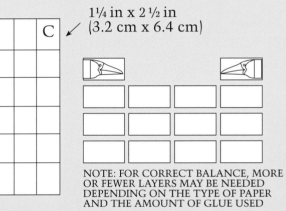

NOTE: FOR CORRECT BALANCE, MORE OR FEWER LAYERS MAY BE NEEDED DEPENDING ON THE TYPE OF PAPER AND THE AMOUNT OF GLUE USED

STEP 13   Using sheet C, measure and cut fourteen small pieces, as shown. On two of the pieces, make a tracing of each side of the booby's head shown on p 32.

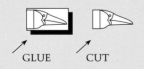

STEP 14   Glue the pieces one on top of the other, having the tracings on the two outer sides, making sure that they are aligned. Then cut out the shape of the head, as shown.

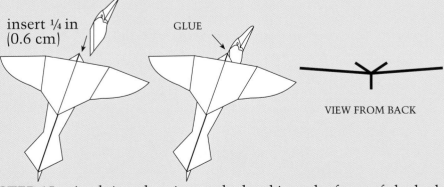

STEP 15   Applying glue, insert the head into the front of the body. Then adjust the dihedral (upward slant of wings), as shown.

Blue-Footed Booby

This paper booby is smaller than actual size. The actual bird is about 25 inches (37.5 cm) in length, with a wingspan of 60 in (100 cm) when fully extended. The plumage coloration of both male and female is similar. The wings and tail are brown. The body is white. The face is also white with a black mask, but prominent is its large blue bill. And as its name suggests, the webbed feet too are blue.

Male and female coloration

32

BIRD MARKINGS PATTERN

NOTE: ADD PATTERN AND COLOR AFTER EACH PART IS COMPLETED, BEFORE FINAL ASSEMBLY

TRACE HEAD TO DOTTED LINE

HEAD IS INSERTED

Canada Goose

This is the most common of all the geese found on the North American continent. Canada geese nest in the many lakes found across the northern portion of the continent. During the winter they are found in southern wetlands and in the coastal regions. Geese fly with slow and steady wingbeats. Their landing is comprised of a long glide, with webbed feet streched out forward like skiis. Slowly they increase the angle of attack until the wings stall just at touchdown. In flight they make a V-formation, with one goose taking the lead, and the rest trailing behind on either side. This has a very practical purpose. Every goose flying ahead of another leaves a slipstream. This is air that rotates upward as it slips around the wingtips. Because this rotating air provides lift, flying in it is less work and therefore less tiring. In this way each individual goose is helping along the entire flock, with the exception of the leader. The lead position is the hardest work because the leader flies in undisturbed air. That is why every so often the leader will move off and take its place at the rear, allowing one of the geese behind to take over. In this way every goose takes its turn at providing added lift for all the others.

After the breeding season, geese congregate in huge colonies, spending the nights near water and flying to open range and farmland for grazing during the day. They are preparing for migration. Juveniles practice flight, and all are fattening up for the long flight south. Just before freeze-up many V-shaped formations can be seen, often at great heights, in migration to the winter feeding grounds. They migrate both day and night, until they reach their destinations.

STEP 1   Measure and cut the various pieces from two sheets of bond paper.

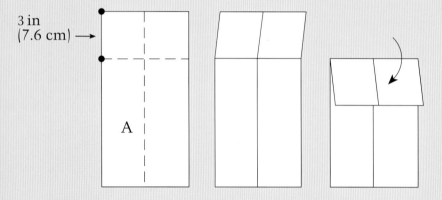

STEP 2   Lay piece A flat in a vertical direction. To make the body, fold in half vertically using a valley fold. Unfold. Measure from top and valley fold, as shown.

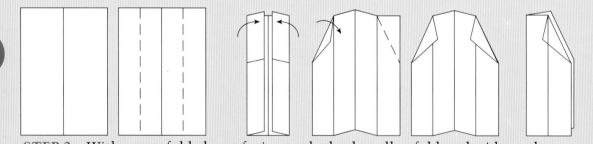

STEP 3   With upper folded part facing to the back, valley fold each side so that outer edges meet center crease, as shown. Unfold. On each side, valley fold diagonally across the folded over section, as shown. Then refold original vertical center crease, as shown.

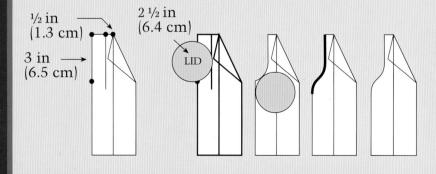

STEP 4   On the left edge, measure from top and make a mark. Along the top edge, from the center crease, measure, mark, and draw a vertical line, as shown. Using the mark on the left edge and the line as guides, trace around a lid. Then move the lid over to round off the second edge, as shown. Cut out the curves, as shown by the heavy line.

34

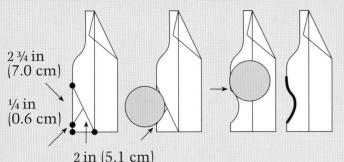

2 ¾ in (7.0 cm)

¼ in (0.6 cm)

2 in (5.1 cm)

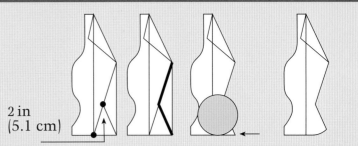

2 in (5.1 cm)

STEP 5   On the left side, measure and draw lines, as shown. Using the drawn lines as an alignment guide, trace around a jar lid and cut rounded corners, as shown by heavy line.

STEP 6   From right-hand corner of diagonal fold, draw a diagonal line to the bottom of vertical center crease. From the bottom, measure along diagonal line and mark. Draw diagonal line from the mark to the bottom right-hand corner. Then cut out, as shown by heavy line. Tracing around a lid, round the tail, as shown.

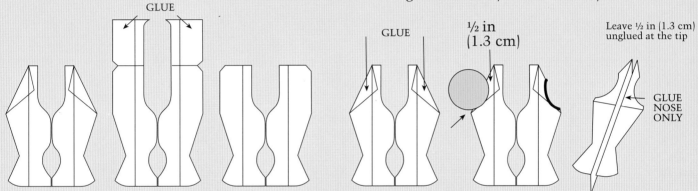

GLUE

GLUE

½ in (1.3 cm)

Leave ½ in (1.3 cm) unglued at the tip

GLUE NOSE ONLY

STEP 7   Unfold body completely. Refold applying glue to all contacting surfaces, as shown. On each side, measure from vertical crease. Then, using the triangular folded over flaps as positioning guides, trace around a lid. Cut out to make the goose's neck, as shown by heavy line. Shape body as shown. Glue nose only, leaving the tip unglued.

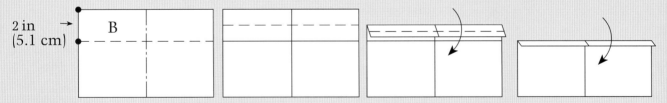

2 in (5.1 cm)

B

STEP 8   Lay piece B horizontally to make the wings. Fold in half vertically, using a mountain fold. Unfold. Measure from top edge and fold horizontally, using a valley fold. Unfold. Then valley fold so that top edge meets horizontal crease. Fold again so that the new top edge meets the horizontal crease. Refold original horizontal crease.

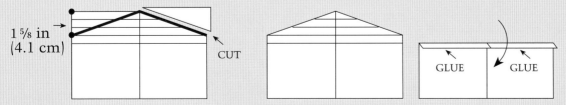

1 ⅝ in (4.1 cm)

CUT

GLUE   GLUE

STEP 9   Unfold completely. On each side, measure and cut diagonally, as shown. Refold. Apply glue before refolding original horizontal center crease only. The folded over part is the bottom of the front edge of the wings.

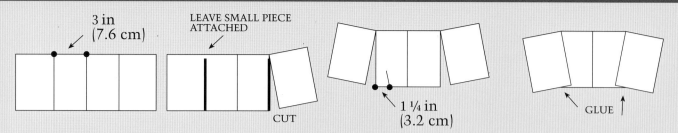

3 in (7.6 cm)

LEAVE SMALL PIECE ATTACHED

CUT

1 ¼ in (3.2 cm)

GLUE

STEP 10 To shape the wings, measure on each side, mark, and draw lines, as shown. Then, on each side, cut from the back edge as shown by heavy lines, leaving a small piece attached at the front edge. From each cut, measure and make a mark on the back edge, as shown. Align outer pieces to the marks. Glue.

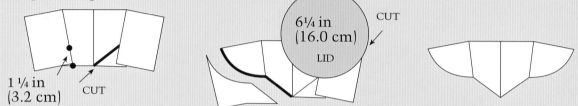

1 ¼ in (3.2 cm) **CUT**

6 ¼ in (16.0 cm) **CUT** **LID**

STEP 11 On each side, measure from the back edge along the glued line and make marks. Then, using the marks and the wingtips, trace around a large lid and cut out to round the wingtips.

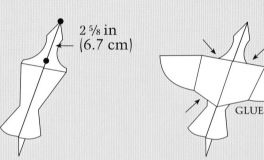

2 ⅝ in (6.7 cm)

GLUE

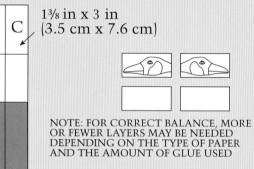

1⅜ in x 3 in (3.5 cm x 7.6 cm)

C

NOTE: FOR CORRECT BALANCE, MORE OR FEWER LAYERS MAY BE NEEDED DEPENDING ON THE TYPE OF PAPER AND THE AMOUNT OF GLUE USED

STEP 12 Measure from front of body and mark for wing position. Glue wings in place, as shown.

STEP 13 Using sheet C, measure and cut four small pieces, as shown. On two of the pieces, make a tracing of each side of the goose's head shown on p 37.

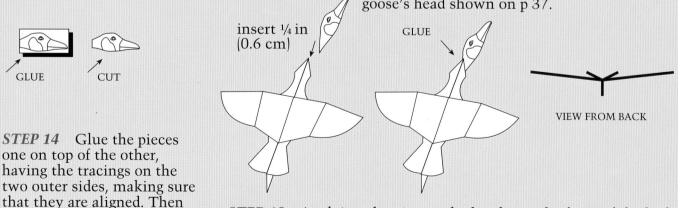

GLUE **CUT**

insert ¼ in (0.6 cm)

GLUE

STEP 14 Glue the pieces one on top of the other, having the tracings on the two outer sides, making sure that they are aligned. Then cut out the shape of the head, as shown.

STEP 15 Applying glue, insert the head into the front of the body. Then adjust the dihedral (upward slant of wings), as shown.

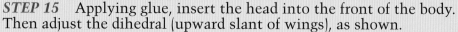

VIEW FROM BACK

Canada Goose

This paper goose is smaller than actual size. The actual goose is about 20 inches (50 cm) in length, with a wingspan of 60 in (150 cm) when fully extended. The coloration of the plumage of both male and female is similar. The black neck and head with distinctive white cheek patches are characteristic of this goose. The wings and back are dark to medium brown. The breast is white, with the rest of the body white to light brown. The tail is black and white.

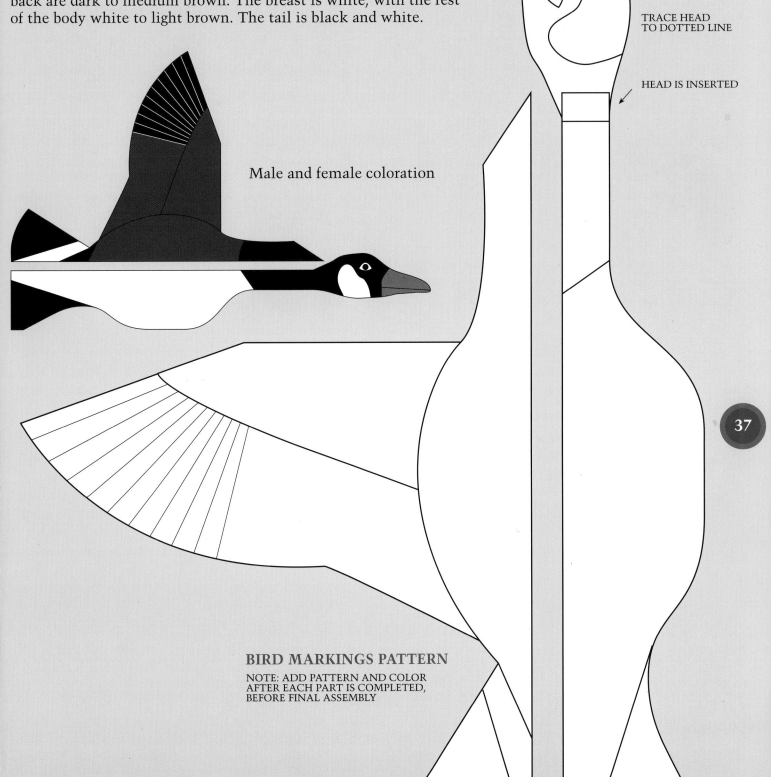

Male and female coloration

TRACE HEAD
TO DOTTED LINE

HEAD IS INSERTED

BIRD MARKINGS PATTERN

NOTE: ADD PATTERN AND COLOR
AFTER EACH PART IS COMPLETED,
BEFORE FINAL ASSEMBLY

37

Cardinal

Cardinals are erratic in their migration and wandering. They are found mainly in the eastern and midwestern regions of North America. They can be seen in hedgerows, the margins of woods, and in the suburban areas of cities. Like other woodland birds, their wings are broad and somewhat rounded. They are fast flyers, and except for landing, don't resort to gliding flight very often. But they are not long distance flyers. Because their entire diet is made up of a variety of seeds, most of their flying is done moving from one source of seeds to another. They nest in trees, shrubs, or even on the ground.

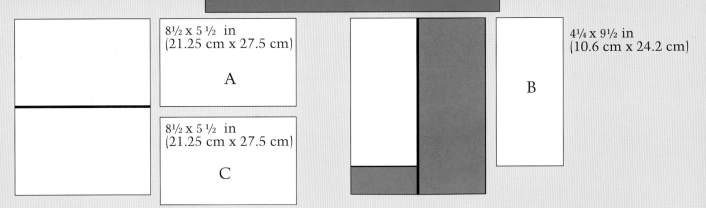

8½ x 5 ½ in
(21.25 cm x 27.5 cm)

A

4¼ x 9½ in
(10.6 cm x 24.2 cm)

B

8½ x 5 ½ in
(21.25 cm x 27.5 cm)

C

STEP 1 Measure and cut the various pieces from two sheets of bond paper.

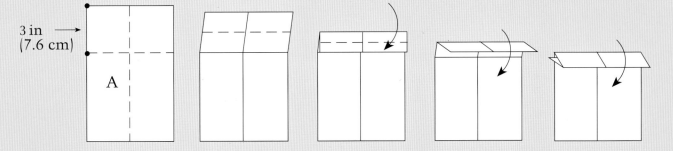

3 in
(7.6 cm)

A

STEP 2 Lay piece A flat in a vertical direction. To make the body, fold in half vertically using a valley fold. Unfold. Measure from top and valley fold, as shown. Unfold. Valley fold top portion so that top edge meets horizontal crease. Then fold top portion again so that top edge meets horizontal crease. Finally, fold over again along original horizontal crease.

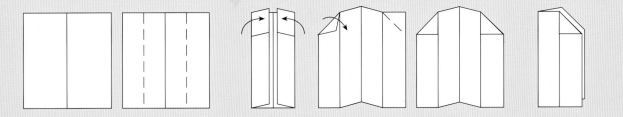

STEP 3 With upper folded part facing to the back, valley fold each side so that outer edges meet center crease, as shown. Unfold. On each side, valley fold diagonally so that top edge meets vertical crease, as shown. Then refold original vertical center crease, as shown.

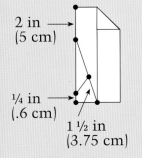

2 in
(5 cm)

¼ in
(.6 cm)

1 ½ in
(3.75 cm)

STEP 4 On the left edge, measure from top and draw diagonal line to bottom center crease. Measure along drawn line from the bottom and mark. On the left edge, measure from bottom and mark. Join the two marks, as shown.

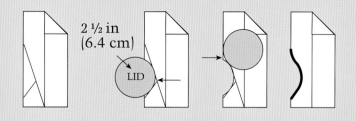
2 ½ in
(6.4 cm)

LID

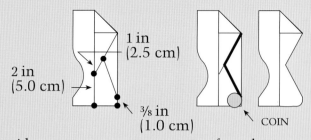
1 in
(2.5 cm)

2 in
(5.0 cm)

⅜ in
(1.0 cm)

COIN

STEP 5 Using the drawn lines as an alignment guide, trace around a jar lid and cut rounded corners, as shown by heavy line.

STEP 6 Along center crease, measure from bottom and mark a point. From right-hand corner of diagonal fold, draw a diagonal line to the point. From point, measure along diagonal line and mark. Along bottom edge, measure from center crease and mark. Draw diagonal line, joining the two marks. Then cut out, as shown by heavy line. Round the bottom right-hand corner by tracing around a coin.

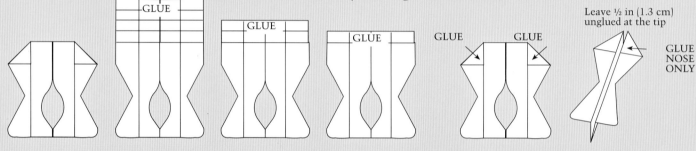
GLUE

GLUE

GLUE

GLUE   GLUE

Leave ½ in (1.3 cm) unglued at the tip

GLUE NOSE ONLY

STEP 7 Unfold body completely. Refold applying glue to all contacting surfaces, as shown. Shape body as shown. Glue nose only, leaving the tip unglued.

B

40

STEP 8 Lay piece B horizontally to make the wings. Fold in half vertically, using a mountain fold. Unfold. Fold in half horizontally, using a valley fold. Unfold. Then valley fold so that top edge meets center crease. Fold again so that the new top edge meets the center crease. Refold original horizontal center crease.

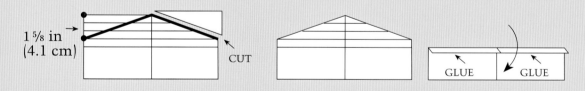
1 ⅝ in
(4.1 cm)

CUT

GLUE   GLUE

STEP 9 Unfold completely. On each side, measure and cut diagonally, as shown. Refold. Apply glue before refolding original horizontal center crease only. The folded over part is the bottom of the front edge of the wings.

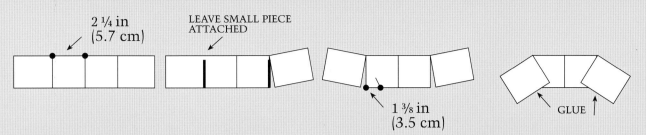

2 ¼ in
(5.7 cm)

LEAVE SMALL PIECE
ATTACHED

1 ⅜ in
(3.5 cm)

GLUE

STEP 10   To shape the wings, measure on each side, mark, and draw lines, as shown. Then, on each side, cut from the back edge as shown by heavy lines, leaving a small piece attached at the front edge. From each cut, measure and make a mark on the back edge, as shown. Align outer pieces to the marks. Glue.

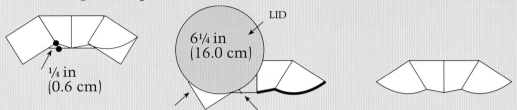

¼ in
(0.6 cm)

LID

6¼ in
(16.0 cm)

STEP 11   On each side, measure from the back edge along the glued line and make a mark, as shown. Draw line from mark to bottom center. To shape the back edge of the wings, trace around the lid (from a cooking pot) aligned with the mark and the outer wingtip and cut out, as shown by heavy line.

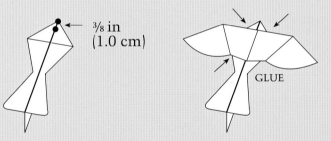

⅜ in
(1.0 cm)

GLUE

1¾ in x 2 ½ in
(4.5 cm x 6.4 cm)

C

NOTE: FOR CORRECT BALANCE, MORE OR FEWER LAYERS MAY BE NEEDED DEPENDING ON THE TYPE OF PAPER AND THE AMOUNT OF GLUE USED

STEP 12   Measure from front of body and mark for wing position. Glue wings in place, as shown.

STEP 13   Using sheet C, measure and cut eight small pieces, as shown. On two of the pieces, make a tracing of each side of the cardinal's head, shown on p 42.

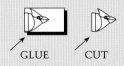

GLUE   CUT

STEP 14   Glue the pieces one on top of the other, having the tracings on the two outer sides, making sure that they are aligned. Then cut out the shape of the head, as shown.

insert ¼ in
(0.6 cm)

GLUE

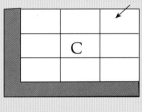

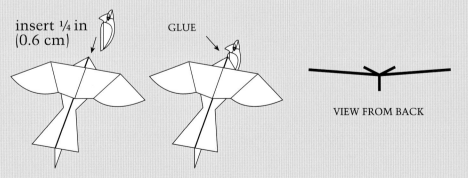

VIEW FROM BACK

STEP 15   Applying glue, insert the head into the front of the body. Then adjust the dihedral (upward slant of wings), as shown.

Cardinal

This paper cardinal is smaller than actual size. The actual cardinal is about 8 inches (20 cm) in length, with a wing span slightly greater when fully extended. The male has a bright red breast. Its wings, tail, and back are a darker red. The female has a yellowish-brown breast with reddish-brown wings, tail, and back. Both have a black mask on the face, although the male's is more pronounced. Both have a conspicuous crest. Their thick bills are red.

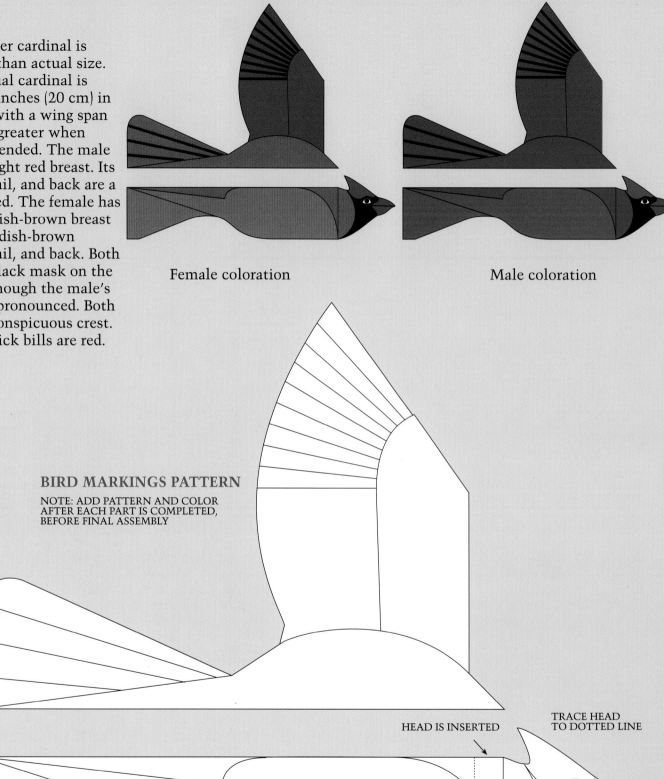

Female coloration

Male coloration

BIRD MARKINGS PATTERN

NOTE: ADD PATTERN AND COLOR AFTER EACH PART IS COMPLETED, BEFORE FINAL ASSEMBLY

42

HEAD IS INSERTED

TRACE HEAD TO DOTTED LINE

Common Loon

Loons give the many lakes of northern North America their distinctive character by filling the air with eerie yodel-like laughter. Loons can often be seen skimming the surface of the water in swift and direct flight, as they move from one spot to another on a lake. Their flight consists of rapid and uninterrupted wingbeats. In flight, they hold their head lower than the body, distinguishing them from other waterfowl. Loons come ashore only for nesting. They are awkward on dry land. Because their feet are so far back, they cannot walk or run upright, but shuffle along sliding on the breastbone. Therefore they are unable to take off from land. To do this they must be in the water, where they paddle and run on the water while flapping their wings to gain enough speed to become airborne. While loons are good flyers, they excel at diving. But unlike boobies that begin their dives while being airborne, loons begin their dives from a swimming position, entering the water with a short forward plunge or sinking, submarine-like, slowly out of sight. They swim considerable distances underwater in pursuit of fish, using their large webbed feet for propulsion.

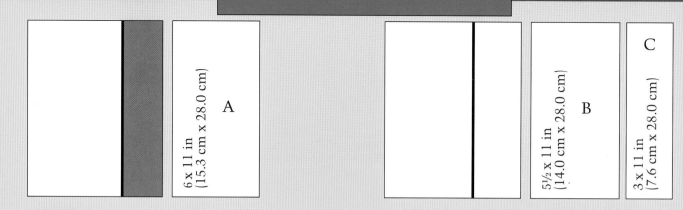

STEP 1 Measure and cut the various pieces from two sheets of bond paper.

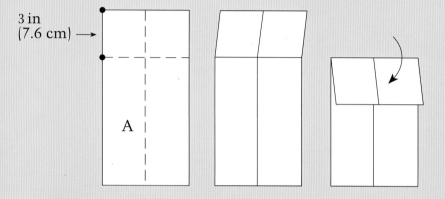

STEP 2 Lay piece A flat in a vertical direction. To make the body, fold in half vertically using a valley fold. Unfold. Measure from top and valley fold, as shown.

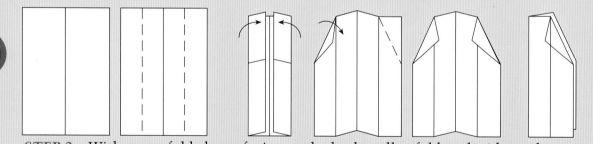

STEP 3 With upper folded part facing to the back, valley fold each side so that outer edges meet center crease, as shown. Unfold. On each side, valley fold diagonally across the folded over section, as shown. Then refold original vertical center crease, as shown.

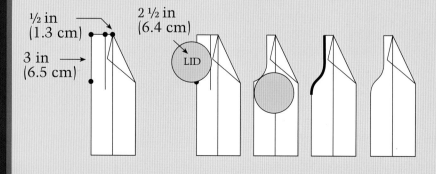

STEP 4 On the left edge, measure from top and make a mark. Along the top edge, from the center crease, measure, mark, and draw a vertical line, as shown. Using the mark on the left edge and the line as guides, trace around a lid. Then move the lid over to round off the second edge, as shown. Cut out the curves, as shown by the heavy line.

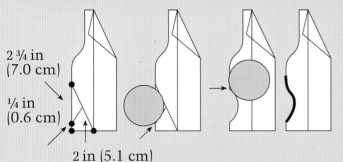

2 ¾ in (7.0 cm)

¼ in (0.6 cm)

2 in (5.1 cm)

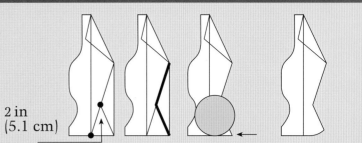

2 in (5.1 cm)

STEP 5   On the left side, measure and draw lines, as shown. Using the drawn lines as an alignment guide, trace around a jar lid and cut rounded corners, as shown by heavy line.

STEP 6   From right-hand corner of diagonal fold, draw a diagonal line to the bottom of vertical center crease. From the bottom, measure along diagonal line and mark. Draw diagonal line from the mark to the bottom right-hand corner. Then cut out, as shown by heavy line. Tracing around a lid, round the tail, as shown.

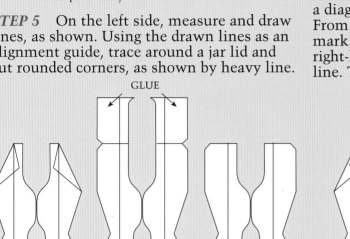

GLUE

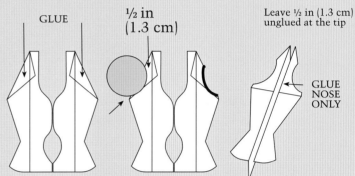

GLUE

½ in (1.3 cm)

Leave ½ in (1.3 cm) unglued at the tip

GLUE NOSE ONLY

STEP 7   Unfold body completely. Refold applying glue to all contacting surfaces, as shown. On each side, measure from vertical crease. Then, using the triangular folded over flaps as positioning guides, trace around a lid. Cut out to make the loon's neck, as shown by heavy line. Shape body as shown. Glue nose only, leaving the tip unglued.

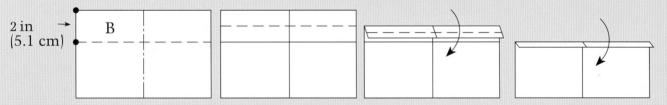

2 in (5.1 cm)

B

STEP 8   Lay piece B horizontally to make the wings. Fold in half vertically, using a mountain fold. Unfold. Measure from top edge and fold horizontally, using a valley fold. Unfold. Then valley fold so that top edge meets horizontal crease. Fold again so that the new top edge meets the horizontal crease. Refold original horizontal crease.

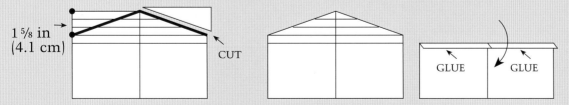

1 ⅝ in (4.1 cm)

CUT

GLUE   GLUE

STEP 9   Unfold completely. On each side, measure and cut diagonally, as shown. Refold. Apply glue before refolding original horizontal center crease only. The folded over part is the bottom of the front edge of the wings.

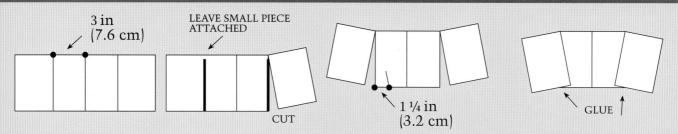

3 in
(7.6 cm)

LEAVE SMALL PIECE
ATTACHED

CUT

1 ¼ in
(3.2 cm)

GLUE

STEP 10   To shape the wings, measure on each side, mark, and draw lines, as shown. Then, on each side, cut from the back edge as shown by heavy lines, leaving a small piece attached at the front edge. From each cut, measure and make a mark on the back edge, as shown. Align outer pieces to the marks. Glue.

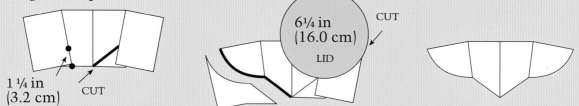

1 ¼ in
(3.2 cm)

CUT

6 ¼ in
(16.0 cm)

CUT

LID

STEP 11   On each side, measure from the back edge along the glued line and make marks. Then, using the marks and the wingtips, trace around a large lid and cut out to round the wingtips.

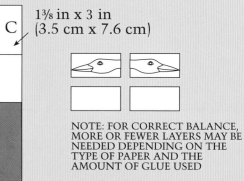

2 ⅝ in
(6.7 cm)

GLUE

C

1 ⅜ in x 3 in
(3.5 cm x 7.6 cm)

NOTE: FOR CORRECT BALANCE, MORE OR FEWER LAYERS MAY BE NEEDED DEPENDING ON THE TYPE OF PAPER AND THE AMOUNT OF GLUE USED

STEP 12   Measure from front of body and mark for wing position. Glue wings in place, as shown.

STEP 13   Using sheet C, measure and cut four small pieces, as shown. On two of the pieces, make a tracing of each side of the loon's head shown on p 47.

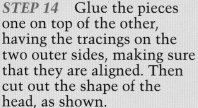

GLUE

CUT

insert ¼ in
(0.6 cm)

GLUE

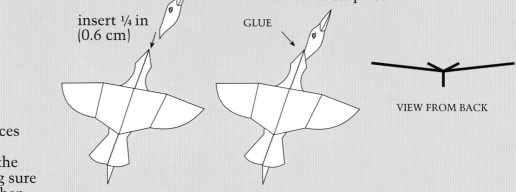

VIEW FROM BACK

STEP 14   Glue the pieces one on top of the other, having the tracings on the two outer sides, making sure that they are aligned. Then cut out the shape of the head, as shown.

STEP 15   Applying glue, insert the head into the front of the body. Then adjust the dihedral (upward slant of wings), as shown.

Common Loon

This paper loon is smaller than actual size. The actual loon is about 22 inches (55 cm) in length, with a wingspan of 58 in (145 cm) when fully extended. The coloration of the plumage of both male and female is similar. The wings and back are black to dark brown, with a distinctive crosshatching in white on the back. The head is black to dark green, with a matching band around the neck. The breast is white, with the rest of the body white to brown. The tapered and pointed bill is black.

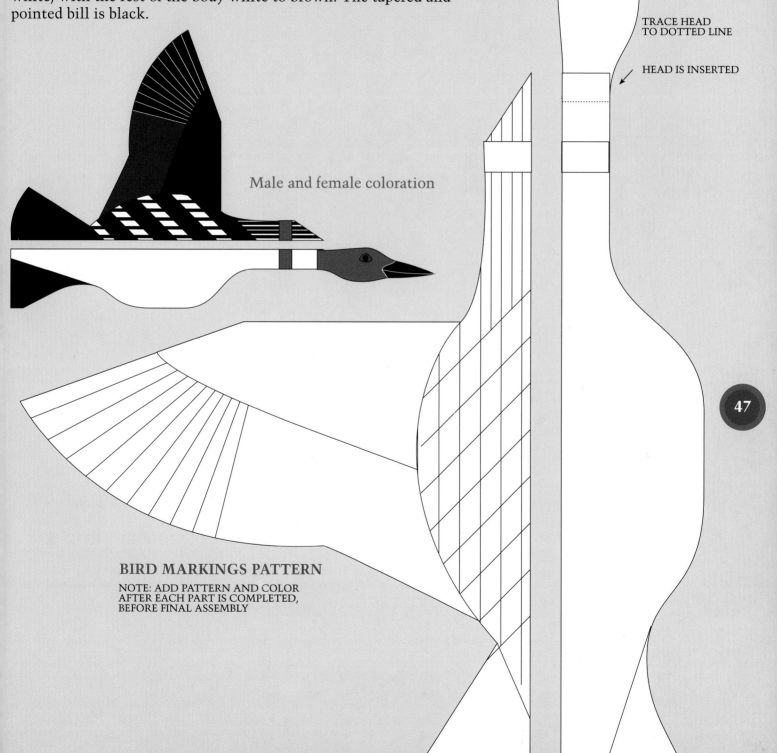

Male and female coloration

BIRD MARKINGS PATTERN

NOTE: ADD PATTERN AND COLOR
AFTER EACH PART IS COMPLETED,
BEFORE FINAL ASSEMBLY

TRACE HEAD
TO DOTTED LINE

HEAD IS INSERTED

47

Flamingo

There is no reason why flamingos need to be good flyers. They don't fly very much for food and they are non-migratory. As it happens, for North American flamingos, food and nesting sites are in one and the same spot. They are found on the mud flats of southern Florida, where they feed on small marine life. The birds' long stilt-like legs and long necks allow them to forage in the shallow water. For nesting, they build low mounds in the shallow water, which gives protection from predators. When they do fly, flamingos are awkward in the air. Their wings are small for the weight of the bird, which makes takeoffs and landings difficult. They need to run a long way to become airborne. Only on the flats can they find such long unobstructed areas. In the air, their long necks are held stretched straight out, counterbalanced by their long legs sticking out to the back. When they come in to land, flamingos approach at high speed, stilt-legs first. Flamingos prefer landing on water where they can use their webbed feet as skies. On dry land they must run in order to slow down from their high-speed approach. Unlike herons, they cannot land in trees. They would crash.

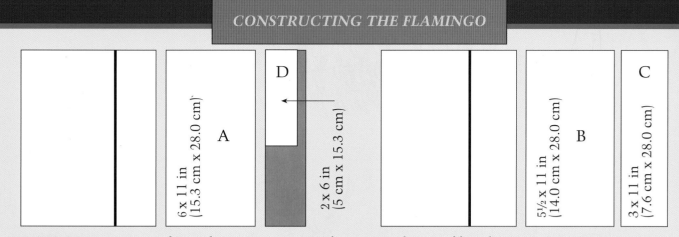

STEP 1 Measure and cut the various pieces from two sheets of bond paper.

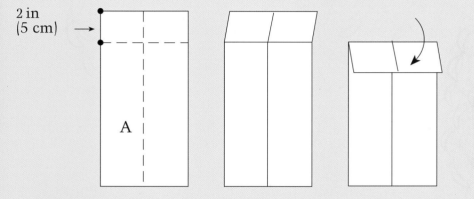

STEP 2 Lay piece A flat in a vertical direction. To make the body, fold in half vertically using a valley fold. Unfold. Measure from top and valley fold, as shown.

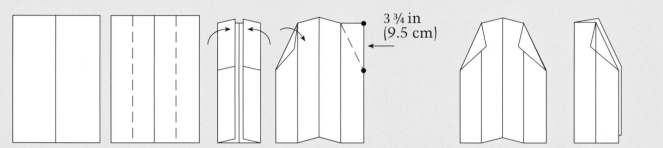

STEP 3 With upper folded part facing to the back, valley fold each side so that outer edges meet center crease, as shown. Unfold. On each side, measure and valley fold diagonally across the folded over section, as shown. Then refold original vertical center crease, as shown.

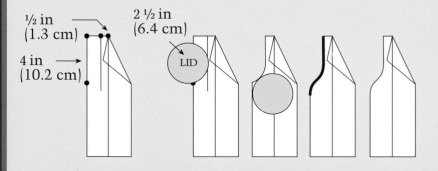

STEP 4 On the left edge, measure from top and make a mark. Along the top edge, from the center crease, measure, mark, and draw a vertical line, as shown. Using the mark on the left edge and the line as guides, trace around a lid. Then move the lid over to round off the second edge, as shown. Cut out the curves, as shown by the heavy line.

49

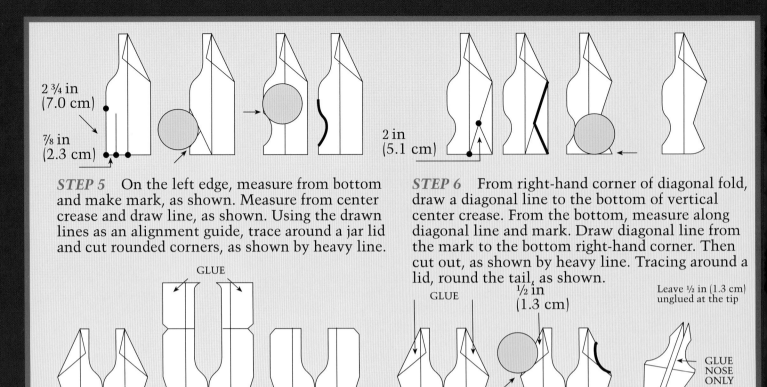

2 ¾ in (7.0 cm)

⅞ in (2.3 cm)

2 in (5.1 cm)

STEP 5   On the left edge, measure from bottom and make mark, as shown. Measure from center crease and draw line, as shown. Using the drawn lines as an alignment guide, trace around a jar lid and cut rounded corners, as shown by heavy line.

STEP 6   From right-hand corner of diagonal fold, draw a diagonal line to the bottom of vertical center crease. From the bottom, measure along diagonal line and mark. Draw diagonal line from the mark to the bottom right-hand corner. Then cut out, as shown by heavy line. Tracing around a lid, round the tail, as shown.

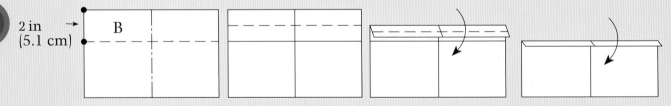

GLUE

GLUE

½ in (1.3 cm)

Leave ½ in (1.3 cm) unglued at the tip

GLUE NOSE ONLY

STEP 7   Unfold body completely. Refold applying glue to all contacting surfaces, as shown. On each side, measure from vertical crease. Then, using the triangular folded over flaps as positioning guides, trace around a lid. Cut out to make the goose's neck, as shown by heavy line. Shape body as shown. Glue nose only, leaving the tip unglued.

2 in (5.1 cm)   B

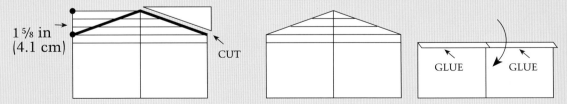

STEP 8   Lay piece B horizontally to make the wings. Fold in half vertically, using a mountain fold. Unfold. Measure from top edge and fold horizontally, using a valley fold. Unfold. Then valley fold so that top edge meets horizontal crease. Fold again so that the new top edge meets the horizontal crease. Refold original horizontal crease.

1 ⅝ in (4.1 cm)

CUT

GLUE   GLUE

STEP 9   Unfold completely. On each side, measure and cut diagonally, as shown. Refold. Apply glue before refolding original horizontal center crease only. The folded over part is the bottom of the front edge of the wings.

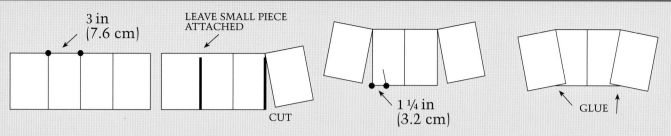

STEP 10 To shape the wings, measure on each side, mark, and draw lines, as shown. Then, on each side, cut from the back edge as shown by heavy lines, leaving a small piece attached at the front edge. From each cut, measure and make a mark on the back edge, as shown. Align outer pieces to the marks. Glue.

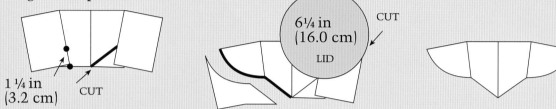

STEP 11 On each side, measure from the back edge along the glued line and make marks. Then, using the marks and the wingtips, trace around a large lid and cut out to round the wingtips.

NOTE: FOR CORRECT BALANCE, MORE OR FEWER LAYERS MAY BE NEEDED DEPENDING ON THE TYPE OF PAPER AND THE AMOUNT OF GLUE USED

1⅜ in x 3 in
(3.5 cm x 7.6 cm)

STEP 13 Using sheet C, measure and cut four small pieces, as shown. On two of the pieces, make a tracing of each side of the flamingo's head shown on p 52.

¼ in (0.6 cm)

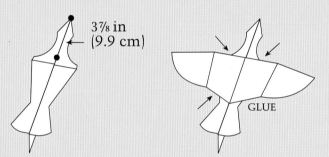

STEP 12 Measure from front of body and mark for wing position. Glue wings in place, as shown.

STEP 15 Use sheet D to make the feet. Valley fold in half horizontally. Measure and cut, as shown by heavy line.

NOTE: THE SIZE OF THE FEET MAY NEED TO BE ADJUSTED TO ACHIEVE BALANCE FOR FLIGHT

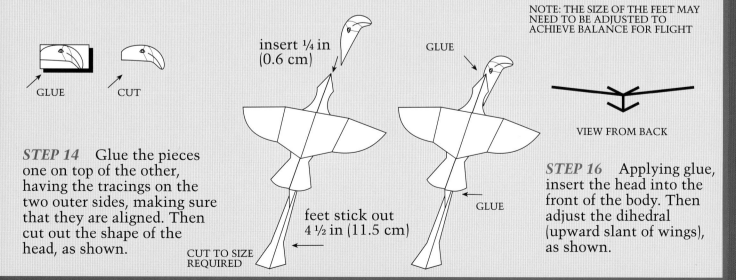

STEP 14 Glue the pieces one on top of the other, having the tracings on the two outer sides, making sure that they are aligned. Then cut out the shape of the head, as shown.

insert ¼ in (0.6 cm)

feet stick out 4 ½ in (11.5 cm)

CUT TO SIZE REQUIRED

VIEW FROM BACK

STEP 16 Applying glue, insert the head into the front of the body. Then adjust the dihedral (upward slant of wings), as shown.

51

Flamingo

This paper flamingo is smaller than actual size. The actual flamingo is about 40 inches (100 cm) in length when in flight with legs extended out the back. It has a wingspan of 55 in (138 cm) when fully extended. The coloration of the plumage of both male and female is similar. The entire bird is pink, ranging from light to deep rose. The color depends on the small red marine life that it eats, which gives the plumage its color. The primary feathers are black. The bill is black and white.

Male and female coloration

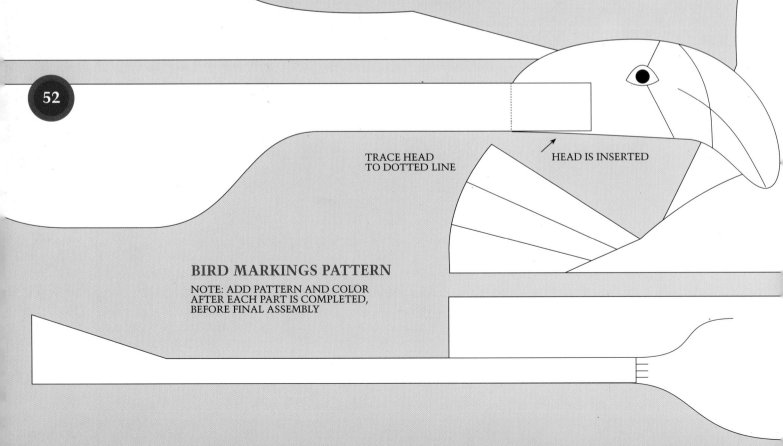

52

TRACE HEAD
TO DOTTED LINE

HEAD IS INSERTED

BIRD MARKINGS PATTERN

NOTE: ADD PATTERN AND COLOR
AFTER EACH PART IS COMPLETED,
BEFORE FINAL ASSEMBLY

Great Horned Owl

The great horned owl's "horns" are not horns at all, they only look like horns. They are actually ear tufts or feathers that stick up.

Owls hunt mainly at night or at dusk. They are especially adapted to night flight. The flight of owls is silent, making them hard to detect by their prey. The wing flapping of most birds can easily be heard because of the air turbulence created. But owls have feathers that are very soft, so that the sound of air turbulence is kept to a minimum. The leading edges of their wings are frayed. Each feather has a layer of short downy fronds that acts as a sound damper. Contibuting to their silent flight is the slowness of their wingbeats and the frequency of glides.

Owls' vision is such that they can see quite well even in the dark, and their hearing is very sharp. Their eyes are large and, unlike those of other birds, are forward facing. The combination of night vision, good hearing, and silent flight makes them a terror for small rodents — their main diet — that scurry about the fields and pastures under the cover of darkness.

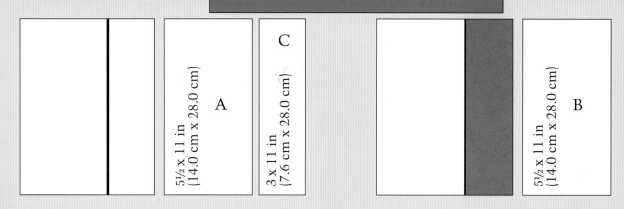

STEP 1   Measure and cut the various pieces from two sheets of bond paper.

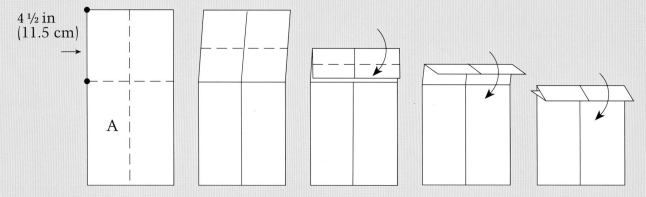

4 ½ in
(11.5 cm)

STEP 2   Lay piece A flat in a vertical direction. To make the body, fold in half vertically using a valley fold. Unfold. Measure from top and valley fold, as shown. Unfold. Valley fold top portion so that top edge meets horizontal crease. Then fold again so that top edge meets horizontal crease. Finally, fold over again along original horizontal crease.

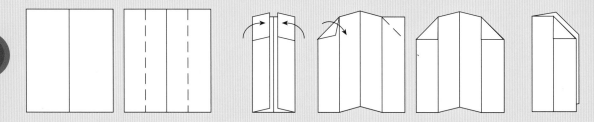

STEP 3   With upper folded part facing to the back, valley fold each side so that outer edges meet center crease, as shown. Unfold. On each side, valley fold diagonally so that top edge meets vertical crease, as shown. Then refold original vertical center crease, as shown.

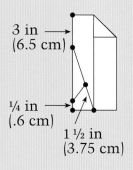

3 in
(6.5 cm)

¼ in
(.6 cm)

1 ½ in
(3.75 cm)

STEP 4   On the left edge, measure from top and draw diagonal line to bottom center crease. Measure along drawn line from the bottom and mark. On the left edge, measure from bottom and mark. Join the two marks, as shown.

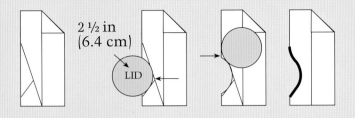
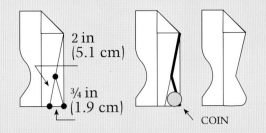

STEP 5   Using the drawn lines as an alignment guide, trace around a jar lid and cut rounded corners, as shown by heavy line.

STEP 6   Along bottom edge, measure from right corner and mark a point. From right-hand corner of diagonal fold, draw a diagonal line to the point. From point, measure along diagonal line and mark. Draw diagonal line from the mark to the bottom right-hand corner. Then cut out, as shown by heavy line. Round bottom right corner by tracing around a coin.

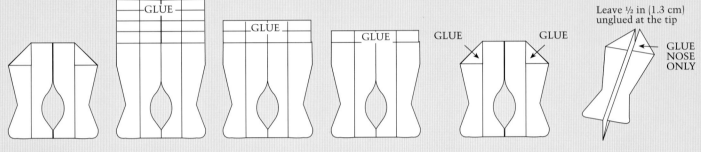

STEP 7   Unfold body completely. Refold applying glue to all contacting surfaces, as shown. Shape body as shown. Glue nose only, leaving the tip unglued.

STEP 8   Lay piece B horizontally to make the wings. Fold in half vertically, using a mountain fold. Unfold. Measure from top edge and fold horizontally, using a valley fold. Unfold. Then valley fold so that top edge meets horizontal crease. Fold again so that the new top edge meets the horizontal crease. Refold original horizontal crease.

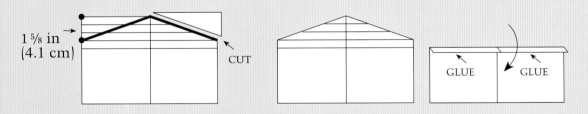

STEP 9   Unfold completely. On each side, measure and cut diagonally, as shown. Refold. Apply glue before refolding original horizontal center crease only. The folded over part is the bottom of the front edge of the wings.

55

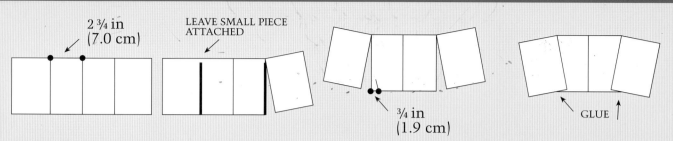

2 ¾ in
(7.0 cm)

LEAVE SMALL PIECE
ATTACHED

¾ in
(1.9 cm)

GLUE

STEP 10   To shape the wings, measure on each side, mark, and draw lines, as shown. Then, on each side, cut from the back edge as shown by heavy lines, leaving a small piece attached at the front edge. From each cut, measure and make a mark on the back edge, as shown. Align outer pieces to the marks. Glue.

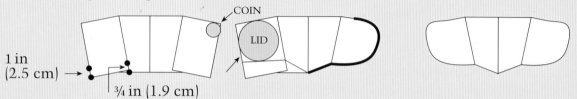

COIN

LID

1 in
(2.5 cm)

¾ in (1.9 cm)

STEP 11   On each side, trace around a coin to round the front corners of the wingtips. Then on each side, measure from the back edge along the glued line and the outer edge, as shown. Draw lines connecting the marks. Using the lines as a positioning guide, trace around a jar lid to round the back corners of the wingtips. Cut out, as shown by heavy line.

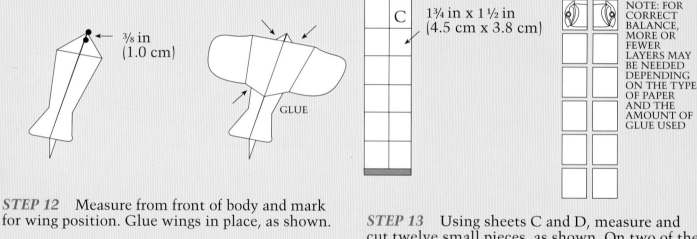

⅜ in
(1.0 cm)

GLUE

C

1 ¾ in x 1 ½ in
(4.5 cm x 3.8 cm)

NOTE: FOR CORRECT BALANCE, MORE OR FEWER LAYERS MAY BE NEEDED DEPENDING ON THE TYPE OF PAPER AND THE AMOUNT OF GLUE USED

STEP 12   Measure from front of body and mark for wing position. Glue wings in place, as shown.

STEP 13   Using sheets C and D, measure and cut twelve small pieces, as shown. On two of the pieces, make a tracing of each side of the owl's head shown on p 57.

GLUE

CUT

GLUE

insert ¼ in
(0.6 cm)

STEP 14   Glue the pieces one on top of the other, having the tracings on the two outer sides, making sure that they are aligned. Then cut out the shape of the head, as shown.

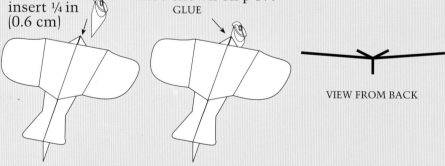

VIEW FROM BACK

STEP 15   Applying glue, insert the head into the front of the body. Then adjust the dihedral (upward slant of wings), as shown.

Great Horned Owl

This paper owl is smaller than actual size. The actual owl is about 20 inches (50 cm) in length, with a wingspan of 55 in (140 cm) when fully extended. The coloration of the plumage of both male and female is a similar streaked or barred white and brown. The overall effect is tawny brown. Its face has the characteristic disk about the eyes. The disk is reddish brown and ringed in black. The ear tufts are brownish.

Male and female coloration

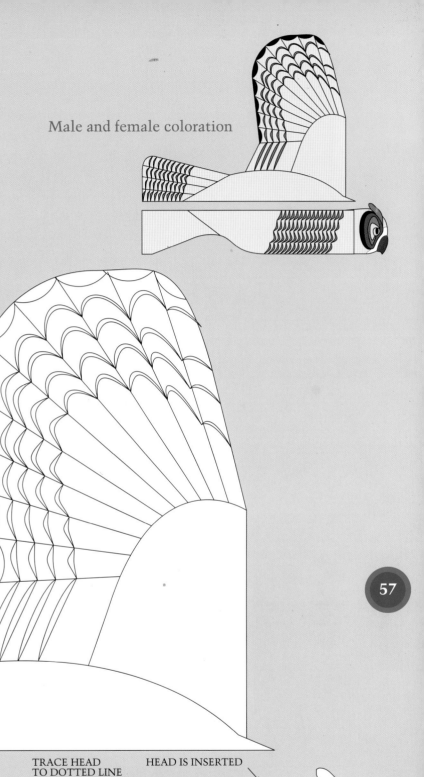

BIRD MARKINGS PATTERN

NOTE: ADD PATTERN AND COLOR
AFTER EACH PART IS COMPLETED,
BEFORE FINAL ASSEMBLY

TRACE HEAD
TO DOTTED LINE

HEAD IS INSERTED

Peregrine Falcon

Falcons are high-speed birds of prey, pursuing other small birds at speeds up to 180 mph (290 kph). They fly with quick powerful wingbeats. At times they soar, especially over the prairies, but they are not known for their soaring ability, as are hawks. Their silhouette shows wings that are long and pointed at the tips and a tail that is almost straight, although it is fanned when soaring. To gain maximum velocity, they partially close their wings to reduce drag and go into a shallow dive. They strike their victims at high speed with their powerful claws, killing them instantly. Falcons are not only swift, but also very maneuverable. During mating season, for example, falcons sometimes share their catches with their mates while on-the-wing. One of the birds briefly turns upside down, the birds going feet-to-feet in mid-air to make the exchange. Falcons sometimes swoop down near the ground to scare up small birds, which they then proceed to tire out in lengthy aerial chases before finally striking them. Even swifts, themselves high-speed flyers, can be captured in this way. At other times falcons will swoop and neatly pick a small perching bird from a branch in a tree or shrub.

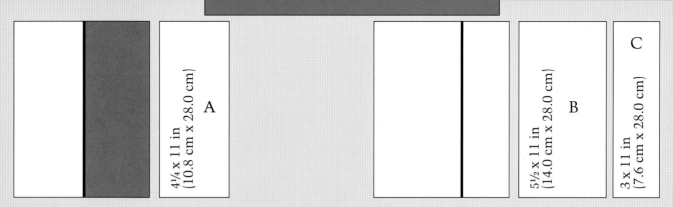

STEP 1   Measure and cut the various pieces from two sheets of bond paper.

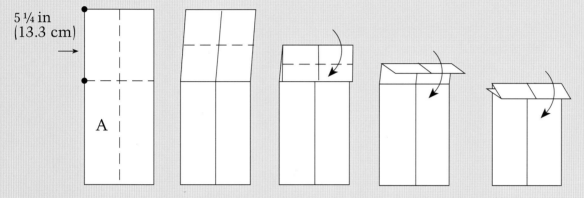

STEP 2   Lay piece A flat in a vertical direction. To make the body, fold in half vertically using a valley fold. Unfold. Measure from top and valley fold, as shown. Unfold. Valley fold top portion so that top edge meets horizontal crease. Then fold top portion again so that top edge meets horizontal crease. Finally, fold over again along original horizontal crease.

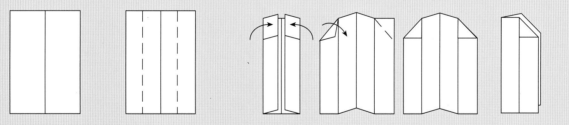

STEP 3   With upper folded part facing to the back, valley fold each side so that outer edges meet center crease, as shown. Unfold. On each side, valley fold diagonally so that top edge meets vertical crease, as shown. Then refold original vertical center crease, as shown.

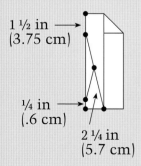

STEP 4   On the left edge, measure from top and draw diagonal line to bottom center crease. Measure along drawn line from the bottom and mark. On the left edge, measure from bottom and mark. Join the two marks, as shown.

59

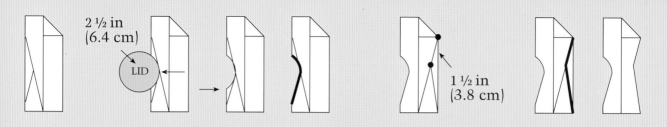

STEP 5 Using the drawn lines as an alignment guide, trace around a jar lid and cut out, as shown by heavy line.

STEP 6 From right-hand corner of diagonal fold, draw a diagonal line to the bottom center crease. From upper point, measure along diagonal line and mark. Draw diagonal line from the mark to the bottom right-hand corner. Then cut out, as shown by heavy line.

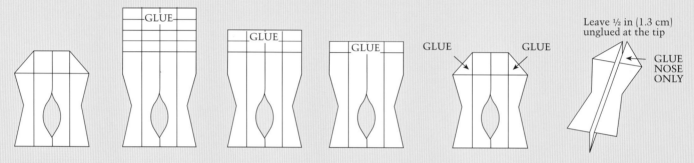

STEP 7 Unfold body completely. Refold applying glue to all contacting surfaces, as shown. Shape body as shown. Glue nose only, leaving the tip unglued.

STEP 8 Lay piece B horizontally to make the wings. Fold in half vertically, using a mountain fold. Unfold. Measure from top edge and fold horizontally, using a valley fold. Unfold. Then valley fold so that top edge meets horizontal crease. Fold again so that the new top edge meets the horizontal crease. Refold original horizontal crease.

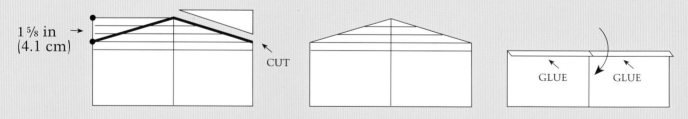

STEP 9 Unfold completely. On each side, measure and cut diagonally, as shown. Refold. Apply glue before refolding original horizontal center crease only. The folded over part is the bottom of the front edge of the wings.

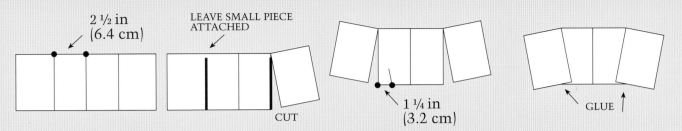

2 ½ in
(6.4 cm)

LEAVE SMALL PIECE
ATTACHED

1 ¼ in
(3.2 cm)

GLUE

CUT

STEP 10 To shape the wings, measure on each side, mark, and draw lines, as shown. Then, on each side, cut from the back edge as shown by heavy lines, leaving a small piece attached at the front edge. From each cut, measure and make a mark on the back edge, as shown. Align outer pieces to the marks. Glue.

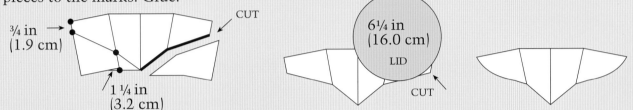

¾ in
(1.9 cm)

CUT

6¼ in
(16.0 cm)
LID

CUT

1 ¼ in
(3.2 cm)

STEP 11 On each side, measure from the back edge along the glued line and the outer edge, make marks. Then draw lines connecting the marks, as shown. Cut along lines. Trace around a large lid and cut out to round the wingtips.

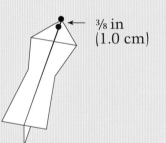

⅜ in
(1.0 cm)

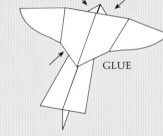

GLUE

C

1½ in x 1 ⅜ in
(3.5 cm x 3.8 cm)

NOTE: FOR CORRECT BALANCE, MORE OR FEWER LAYERS MAY BE NEEDED DEPENDING ON THE TYPE OF PAPER AND THE AMOUNT OF GLUE USED

STEP 12 Measure from front of body and mark for wing position. Glue wings in place, as shown.

STEP 13 Using sheet C, measure and cut twelve small pieces, as shown. On two of the pieces, make a tracing of each side of the falcon's head shown on p 62.

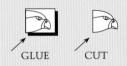

GLUE   CUT

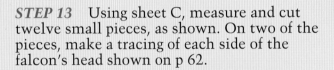

insert ¼ in
(0.6 cm)

GLUE

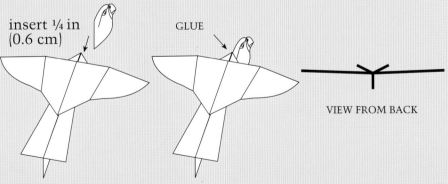

VIEW FROM BACK

STEP 14 Glue the pieces one on top of the other, having the tracings on the two outer sides, making sure that they are aligned. Then cut out the shape of the head, as shown.

STEP 15 Applying glue, insert the head into the front of the body. Then adjust the dihedral (upward slant of wings), as shown.

61

Peregrine Falcon

This paper falcon is smaller than actual size. The actual falcon is about 15 inches (37.5 cm) in length, with a wingspan of 40 in (100 cm) when fully extended. The coloration of the plumage of both male and female is similar. The back and tail are dark brownish gray with light colored bands. The head is capped in black. The face is white. The hooked bill is gray.

Male and female coloration

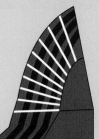

62

BIRD MARKINGS PATTERN

NOTE: ADD PATTERN AND COLOR
AFTER EACH PART IS COMPLETED,
BEFORE FINAL ASSEMBLY

HEAD IS INSERTED   TRACE HEAD
TO DOTTED LINE

Red-Tailed Hawk

Hawks are soaring birds. They prefer gliding flight over flapping flight. Because their wings are large, the birds would become fatigued if they had to flap their wings for long periods of time. Red-tailed hawks can often be seen several hundred feet above the ground, wings outstretched, flying in a current of rising air. They circle overhead and upon sighting prey on the ground, descend in a steep and swift dive, grabbing their prey in their claws. Soaring flight is very well suited to their hunting methods because they feed mainly on small rodents. However, they also soar for the sheer fun of it. When they are not hunting they are sometimes found in thermals many thousands of feet from the ground. They nest in the borders of woodlots near open fields. During the summer months, red-tailed hawks can be found across the North American continent. They winter in the southern regions, migrating in loosely formed flocks together with other kinds of hawks, using thermal and ridge lift to get there.

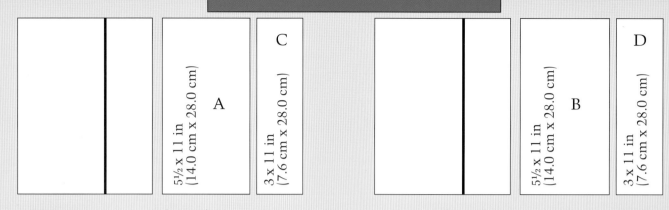

STEP 1 Measure and cut the various pieces from two sheets of bond paper.

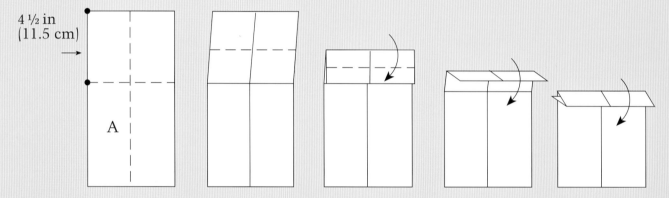

STEP 2 Lay piece A flat in a vertical direction. To make the body, fold in half vertically using a valley fold. Unfold. Measure from top and valley fold, as shown. Unfold. Valley fold top portion so that top edge meets horizontal crease. Then fold top portion again so that top edge meets horizontal crease. Finally, fold over again along original horizontal crease.

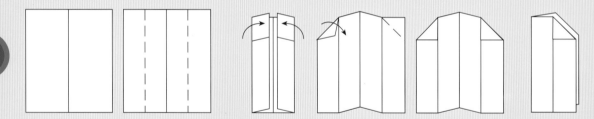

STEP 3 With upper folded part facing to the back, valley fold each side so that outer edges meet center crease, as shown. Unfold. On each side, valley fold diagonally so that top edge meets vertical crease, as shown. Then refold original vertical center crease, as shown.

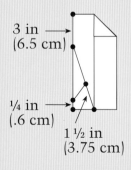

STEP 4 On the left edge, measure from top and draw diagonal line to bottom center crease. Measure along drawn line from the bottom and mark. On the left edge, measure from bottom and mark. Join the two marks, as shown.

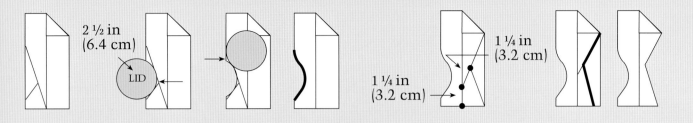

STEP 5 Using the drawn lines as an alignment guide, trace around a jar lid and cut rounded corners, as shown by heavy line.

STEP 6 Along center crease, measure from bottom and mark a point. From right-hand corner of diagonal fold, draw a diagonal line to the point. From point, measure along diagonal line and mark. Draw diagonal line from the mark to the bottom right-hand corner. Then cut out, as shown by heavy line.

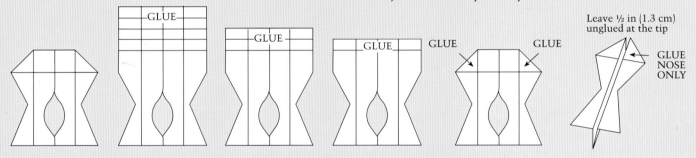

STEP 7 Unfold body completely. Refold applying glue to all contacting surfaces, as shown. Shape body as shown. Glue nose only, leaving the tip unglued.

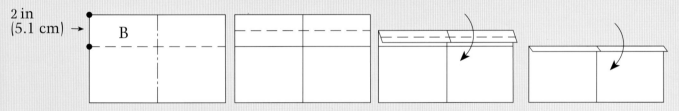

STEP 8 Lay piece B horizontally to make the wings. Fold in half vertically, using a mountain fold. Unfold. Measure from top edge and fold horizontally, using a valley fold. Unfold. Then valley fold so that top edge meets horizontal crease. Fold again so that the new top edge meets the horizontal crease. Refold original horizontal crease.

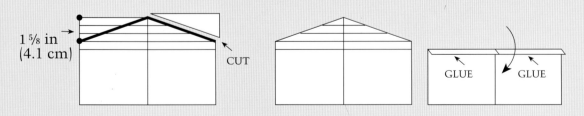

STEP 9 Unfold completely. On each side, measure and cut diagonally, as shown. Refold. Apply glue before refolding original horizontal center crease only. The folded over part is the bottom of the front edge of the wings.

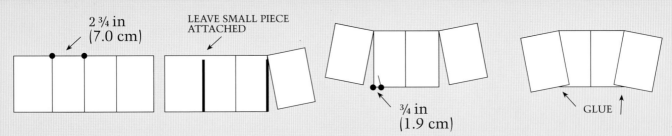

2 ¾ in (7.0 cm)

LEAVE SMALL PIECE ATTACHED

¾ in (1.9 cm)

GLUE

STEP 10 To shape the wings, measure on each side, mark, and draw lines, as shown. Then, on each side, cut from the back edge as shown by heavy lines, leaving a small piece attached at the front edge. From each cut, measure and make a mark on the back edge, as shown. Align outer pieces to the marks. Glue.

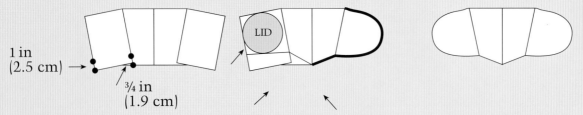

1 in (2.5 cm)

LID

¾ in (1.9 cm)

STEP 11 On each side, measure from the back edge along the glued line and the outer edge, as shown. Then draw lines connecting the marks. Using the lines as a positioning guide, trace around a jar lid to round the wingtips. Cut out, as shown by heavy line.

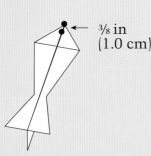

⅜ in (1.0 cm)

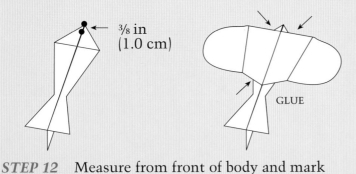

GLUE

C D

1 ¾ in x 2 ½ in (4.5 cm x 6.4 cm)

NOTE: FOR CORRECT BALANCE, MORE OR FEWER LAYERS MAY BE NEEDED DEPENDING ON THE TYPE OF PAPER AND THE AMOUNT OF GLUE USED

STEP 12 Measure from front of body and mark for wing position. Glue wings in place, as shown.

STEP 13 Using sheets C and D, measure and cut twelve small pieces, as shown. On two of the pieces, make a tracing of each side of the hawk's head shown on p 67.

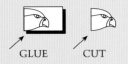

GLUE CUT

STEP 14 Glue the pieces one on top of the other, having the tracings on the two outer sides, making sure that they are aligned. Then cut out the shape of the head, as shown.

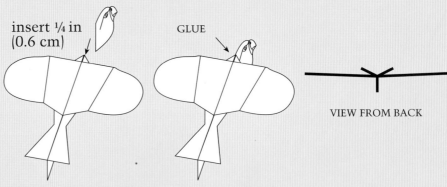

insert ¼ in (0.6 cm)

GLUE

VIEW FROM BACK

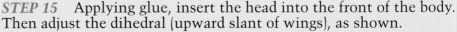

STEP 15 Applying glue, insert the head into the front of the body. Then adjust the dihedral (upward slant of wings), as shown.

66

Red-Tailed Hawk

This paper hawk is smaller than actual size. The actual hawk is about 18 inches (46 cm) in length, with a wingspan of 48 in (122.7 cm) when fully extended. The coloration of the plumage of both male and female is similar, but varies greatly among hawks from streaked white to deep tan. But the darker belly bands always remain, and the tail is always uniformly reddish. The hooked bill is yellowish gray.

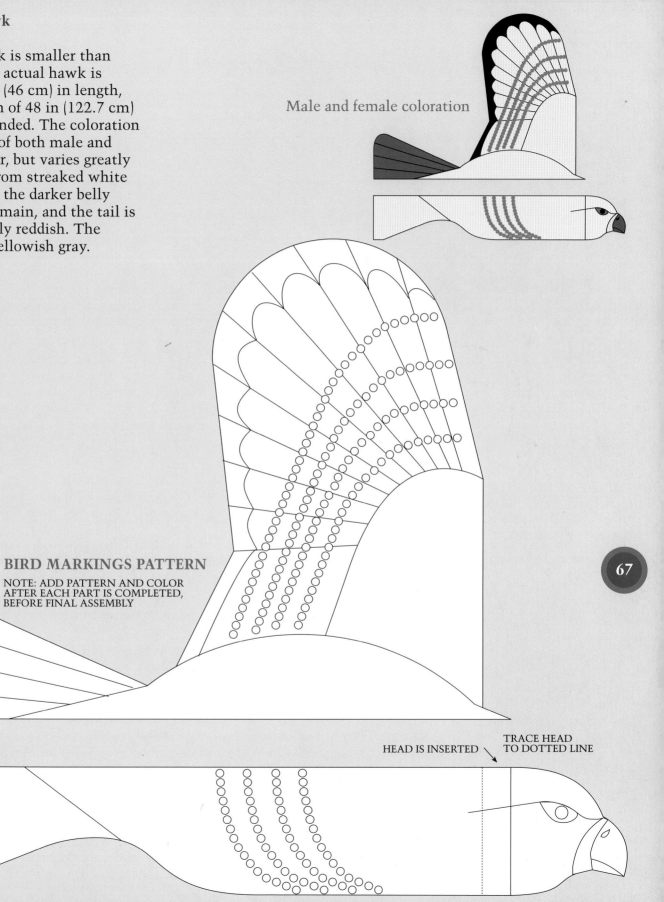

Male and female coloration

BIRD MARKINGS PATTERN

NOTE: ADD PATTERN AND COLOR
AFTER EACH PART IS COMPLETED,
BEFORE FINAL ASSEMBLY

HEAD IS INSERTED

TRACE HEAD
TO DOTTED LINE

Robin

Robins fly with steady wingbeats for propulsion, interspersed with short glides, but they are not soaring birds. In unhurried flight they flap their wings on average 2.3 times each second. Since they live in close proximity to people, we are not particularily aware of robins in flight, except when a parent bird noisily chases an intruder from its nesting area or in the autumn when large flocks congregate for migration.

Robins are many people's favorite birds. Their song is clear and cheerful. Their preferred habitat is woodlots, shrubbery, and open grassy areas. They nest in nearby trees or in nooks on buildings. Their nests are made of grass and twigs smeared with mud and lined with fine grasses and plant down. Robins' most interesting and endearing characteristics are their friendly behavior in the yard or garden. They are often seen on lawns searching for insects and worms, their main diet. To the annoyance of gardeners, they are also fond of fruits and vegetables.

Robins are found south to Central America and as far north as the tree line of Canada's arctic. Those in the north migrate south for the winter just as far as necessary to find a reliable supply of food, returning in the spring before the snow is completely gone. They migrate in flocks, flying only in the daytime. Those in the south migrate north for nesting in the summertime. Over a large part of the United States robins are permanent residents. In northern regions they are often seen as harbingers of spring.

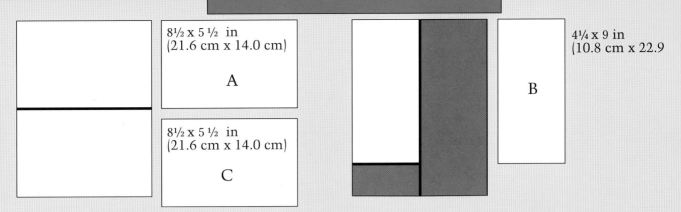

8½ x 5 ½ in
(21.6 cm x 14.0 cm)

A

8½ x 5 ½ in
(21.6 cm x 14.0 cm)

C

B

4¼ x 9 in
(10.8 cm x 22.9

STEP 1   Measure and cut the various pieces from two sheets of bond paper.

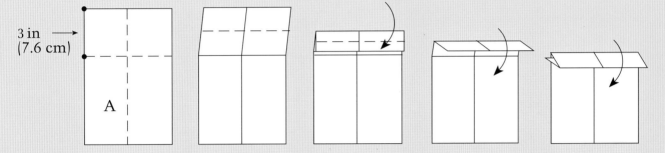

3 in
(7.6 cm)

A

STEP 2   Lay piece A flat in a vertical direction. To make the body, fold in half vertically using a valley fold. Unfold. Measure from top and valley fold, as shown. Unfold. Valley fold top portion so that top edge meets horizontal crease. Then fold top portion again so that top edge meets horizontal crease. Finally, fold over again along original horizontal crease.

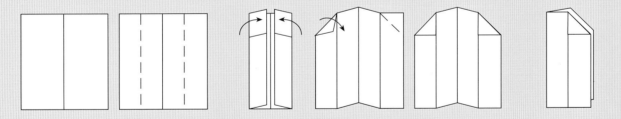

STEP 3   With upper folded part facing to the back, valley fold each side so that outer edges meet center crease, as shown. Unfold. On each side, valley fold diagonally so that top edge meets vertical crease, as shown. Then refold original vertical center crease, as shown.

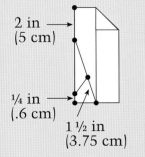

2 in
(5 cm)

¼ in
(.6 cm)

1 ½ in
(3.75 cm)

STEP 4   On the left edge, measure from top and draw diagonal line to bottom center crease. Measure along drawn line from the bottom and mark. On the left edge, measure from bottom and mark. Join the two marks, as shown.

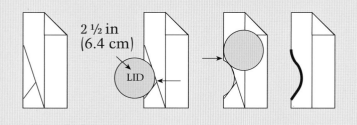 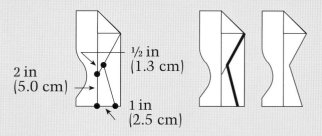

STEP 5   Using the drawn lines as an alignment guide, trace around a jar lid and cut rounded corners, as shown by heavy line.

STEP 6   Along center crease, measure from bottom and mark a point. From right-hand corner of diagonal fold, draw a diagonal line to the point. From point, measure along diagonal line and mark. Along bottom edge, measure from center crease and mark. Draw diagonal line , joining the two marks. Then cut out, as shown by heavy line.

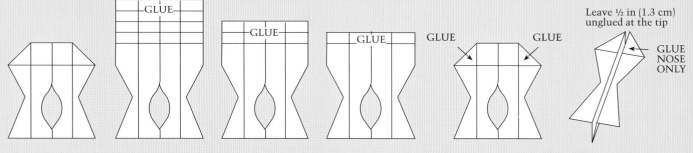

STEP 7   Unfold body completely. Refold applying glue to all contacting surfaces, as shown. Shape body as shown. Glue nose only, leaving the tip unglued.

STEP 8   Lay piece B horizontally to make the wings. Fold in half vertically, using a mountain fold. Unfold. Fold in half horizontally, using a valley fold. Unfold. Then valley fold so that top edge meets center crease. Fold again so that the new top edge meets the center crease. Refold original horizontal center crease.

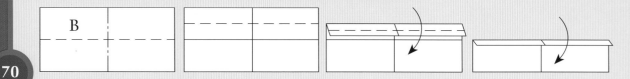

STEP 9   Unfold completely. On each side, measure and cut diagonally, as shown. Refold. Apply glue before refolding original horizontal center crease only. The folded over part is the bottom of the front edge of the wings.

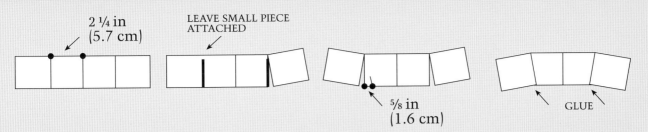

2 ¼ in
(5.7 cm)

LEAVE SMALL PIECE
ATTACHED

⅝ in
(1.6 cm)

GLUE

STEP 10   To shape the wings, measure on each side, mark, and draw lines, as shown. Then, on each side, cut from the back edge as shown by heavy lines, leaving a small piece attached at the front edge. From each cut, measure and make a mark on the back edge, as shown. Align outer pieces to the marks. Glue.

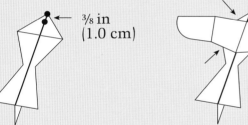

2 ½ in (6.4 cm)

LID

⅝ in
(1.6 cm)

⅜ in
(1.0 cm)

STEP 11   On each side, measure from the back edge along the glued line and the outer edge, as shown. Then draw lines connecting the marks, as shown. Using lines as positioning guides, trace around a jar lid to round the back corners of the wings. Cut out, as shown by heavy line.

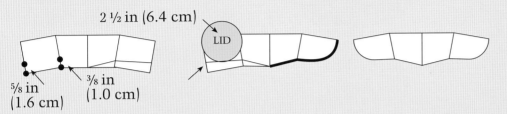

⅜ in
(1.0 cm)

GLUE

1 ½ in x 2 ½ in
(3.8 cm x 6.4 cm)

C

NOTE: FOR CORRECT BALANCE, MORE OR FEWER LAYERS MAY BE NEEDED DEPENDING ON THE TYPE OF PAPER AND THE AMOUNT OF GLUE USED

STEP 12   Measure from front of body and mark for wing position. Glue wings in place, as shown.

STEP 13   Using sheet C, measure and cut eight small pieces, as shown. On two of the pieces, make a tracing of each side of the robin's head shown on p 72.

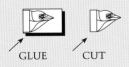

GLUE   CUT

STEP 14   Glue the pieces one on top of the other, having the tracings on the two outer sides, making sure that they are aligned. Then cut out the shape of the head, as shown.

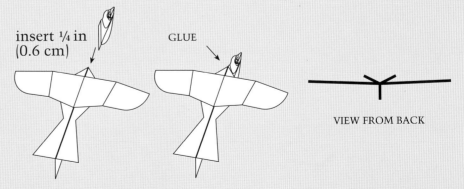
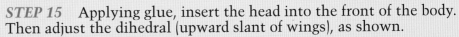

insert ¼ in
(0.6 cm)

GLUE

VIEW FROM BACK

STEP 15   Applying glue, insert the head into the front of the body. Then adjust the dihedral (upward slant of wings), as shown.

71

Robin

This paper robin is smaller than actual size. The actual robin is about 9 inches (23 cm) in length, with a wing span slightly greater when fully extended. Both male and female are similar in coloration, but the female is duller and paler. The top of the head is black, with small white patches around the eyes. The rest of the upper parts of the body and wings are mostly dark gray, becoming nearly black on the wings and tail. The outer tips of the tail are white. The throat is streaked white and black. The rear of the abdomen and under the tail is white. The breast and upper abdomen are brick red. The eyes are brown and the bill is yellow.

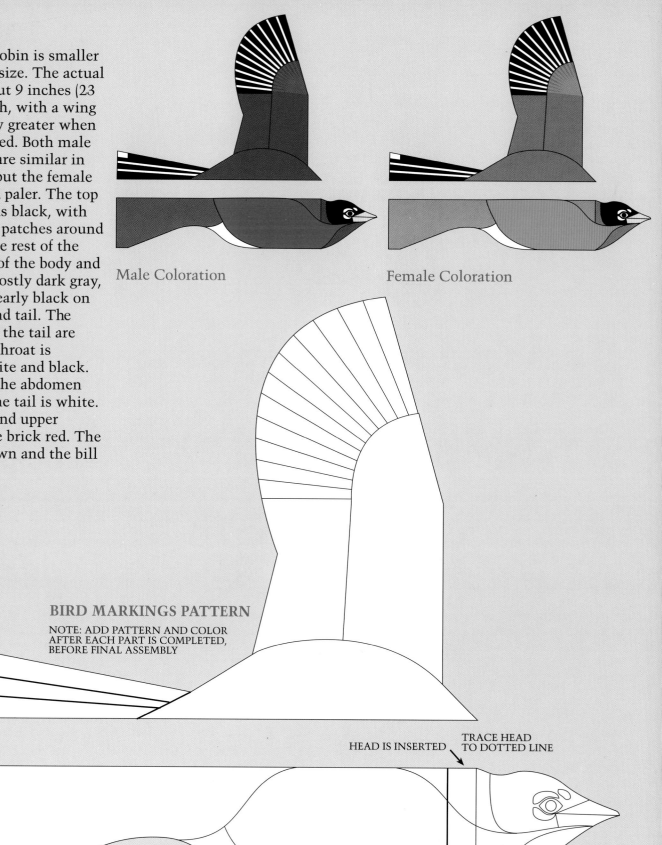

Male Coloration

Female Coloration

BIRD MARKINGS PATTERN

NOTE: ADD PATTERN AND COLOR
AFTER EACH PART IS COMPLETED,
BEFORE FINAL ASSEMBLY

HEAD IS INSERTED

TRACE HEAD
TO DOTTED LINE

Ruddy Turnstone

Turnstones are birds of the high arctic regions of the world. For North American turnstones, this means their summer nesting homes are in Canada's north. They are seen most often running and wading along tidal shorelines in search of food. As their name suggests, they look under and among the beach pebbles for invertebrate marine life. Kelp piles washed up on the shores are other favorite spots. With their sharply tapered wings and stout tails they are good flyers, which their habitat of vast expanses of ocean coastline demands. They fly with fairly rapid and steady wingbeats, gliding mainly upon landing. In the fall some turnstones undertake an extraordinarily long migration flight, following either the Atlantic or Pacific coastline, south as far as the coast of Brazil or the southern tip of Chile for the winter. Others winter all along the Atlantic and Pacific coasts. By the beginning of June turnstones are back in the high arctic again, many having flown a round trip of some 19,000 miles (30,000 kilometers).

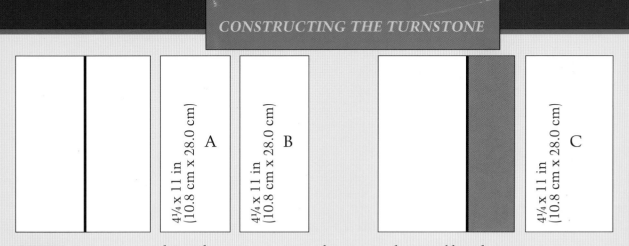

STEP 1 Measure and cut the various pieces from two sheets of bond paper.

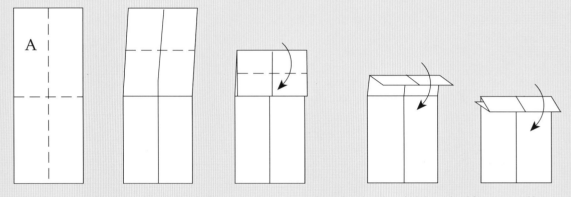

STEP 2 Lay piece A flat in a vertical direction. To make the body, fold in half vertically using a valley fold. Unfold. Fold in half horizontally using a valley fold. Unfold. Valley fold top portion so that top edge meets horizontal crease. Then fold top portion again so that top edge meets horizontal crease. Finally, fold over again along original horizontal crease.

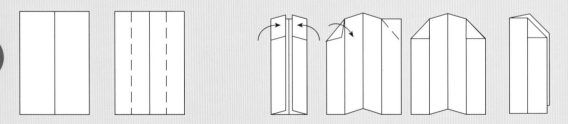

STEP 3 With upper folded part facing to the back, valley fold each side so that outer edges meet center crease, as shown. Unfold. On each side, valley fold diagonally so that top edge meets vertical crease, as shown. Then refold original vertical center crease, as shown.

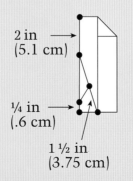

STEP 4 On the left edge, measure from top and draw diagonal line to bottom center crease. Measure along drawn line from the bottom and mark. On the left edge, measure from bottom and mark. Join the two marks, as shown.

74

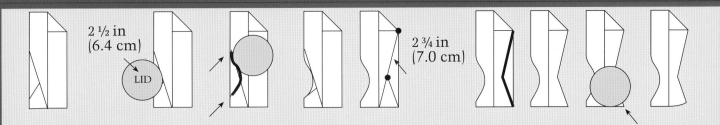

STEP 5   Using the drawn lines as an alignment guide, trace around a jar lid and cut out, as shown by heavy line.

STEP 6   From right-hand corner of diagonal fold, draw a diagonal line to the bottom center crease. From upper point, measure along diagonal line and mark. Draw diagonal line from the mark to the bottom right-hand corner. Cut out, as shown by heavy line. Then trace around a lid to round tail, as shown.

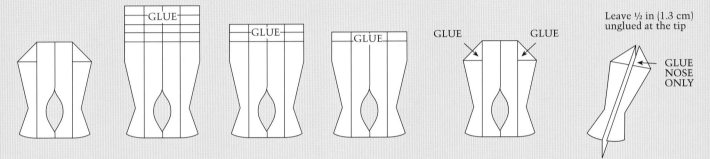

STEP 7   Unfold body completely. Refold applying glue to all contacting surfaces, as shown. Shape body as shown. Glue nose only, leaving the tip unglued.

STEP 8   Lay piece C horizontally to make the wings. Fold in half vertically, using a mountain fold. Unfold. Measure from top edge and fold horizontally, using a valley fold. Unfold. Then valley fold so that top edge meets horizontal crease. Fold again so that the new top edge meets the horizontal crease. Refold original horizontal crease.

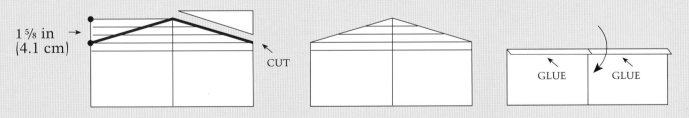

STEP 9   Unfold completely. On each side, measure and cut diagonally, as shown. Refold. Apply glue before refolding original horizontal center crease only. The folded over part is the bottom of the front edge of the wings.

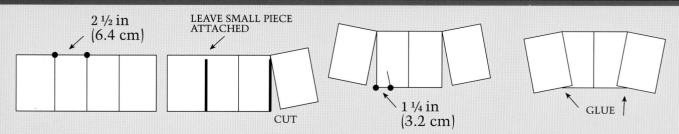

2 ½ in
(6.4 cm)

LEAVE SMALL PIECE
ATTACHED

CUT

1 ¼ in
(3.2 cm)

GLUE

STEP 10 To shape the wings, measure on each side, mark, and draw lines, as shown. Then, on each side, cut from the back edge as shown by heavy lines, leaving a small piece attached at the front edge. From each cut, measure and make a mark on the back edge, as shown. Align outer pieces to the marks. Glue.

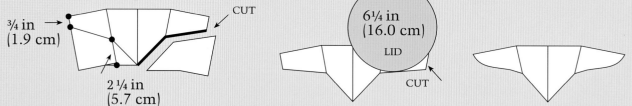

¾ in
(1.9 cm)

CUT

2 ¼ in
(5.7 cm)

6¼ in
(16.0 cm)

LID

CUT

STEP 11 On each side, measure from the back edge along the glued line and the outer edge, make marks. Then draw lines connecting the marks, as shown. Cut along lines. Trace around a large lid and cut out to round the wingtips.

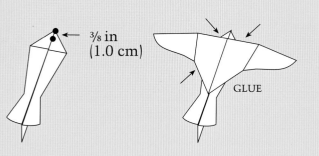

⅜ in
(1.0 cm)

GLUE

B

1¼ in x 2¼ in
(3.2 cm x 5.7 cm)

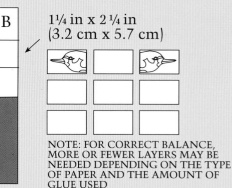

NOTE: FOR CORRECT BALANCE, MORE OR FEWER LAYERS MAY BE NEEDED DEPENDING ON THE TYPE OF PAPER AND THE AMOUNT OF GLUE USED

STEP 12 Measure from front of body and mark for wing position. Glue wings in place, as shown.

STEP 13 Using sheet B, measure and cut nine small pieces, as shown. On two of the pieces, make a tracing of each side of the turnstone's head shown on p 77.

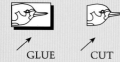

GLUE

CUT

STEP 14 Glue the pieces one on top of the other, having the tracings on the two outer sides, making sure that they are aligned. Then cut out the shape of the head, as shown.

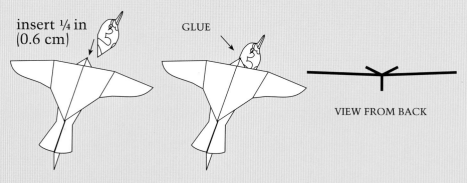

insert ¼ in
(0.6 cm)

GLUE

VIEW FROM BACK

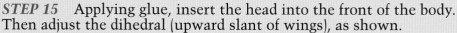

STEP 15 Applying glue, insert the head into the front of the body. Then adjust the dihedral (upward slant of wings), as shown.

Ruddy Turnstone

This paper turnstone is almost actual size. The ruddy turnstone is about 7 inches (17.7 cm) in length, with a wingspan of 15 in (38 cm) when fully extended. The coloration of the plumage of both male and female is similar. Both have a striking black, white, and brown pattern. The breast is white. The back and the outline of the covert feathers is brown. The wings and tail are outlined in black. A striking black face mask extends down the breast and up over the back. The slender bill is dark gray.

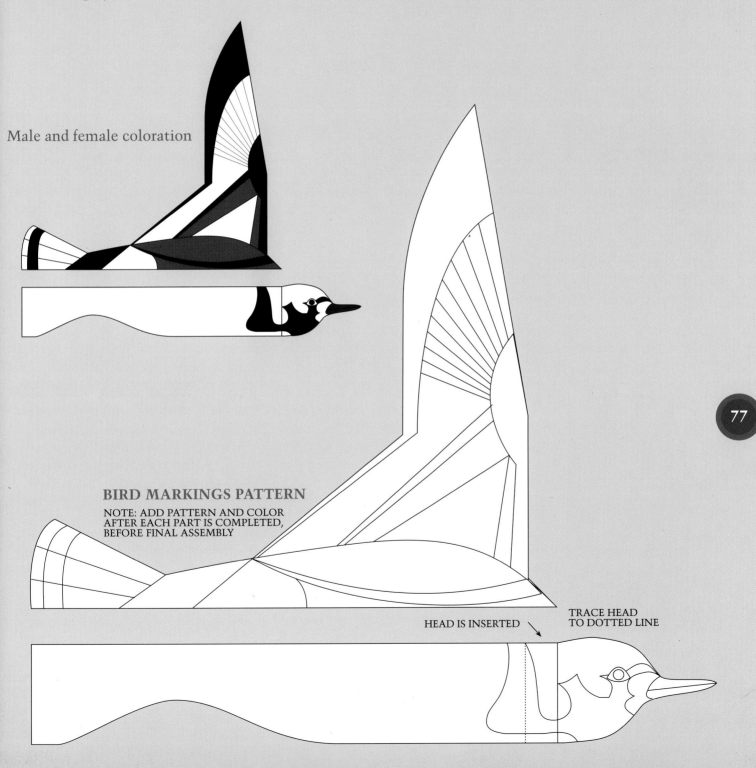

Male and female coloration

BIRD MARKINGS PATTERN

NOTE: ADD PATTERN AND COLOR
AFTER EACH PART IS COMPLETED,
BEFORE FINAL ASSEMBLY

HEAD IS INSERTED

TRACE HEAD
TO DOTTED LINE

Vaux's Swift

Swifts are well named. Of all birds, along with falcons, they are among the fastest flying. Their wings are designed for speed. They are long and slender, stiff and slightly curved, coming to a point at the tips. Swifts often dart about the sky with rapid wing beats. But they also soar on air currents without beating their wings at all. They cruise at high speed covering great distances in search of food. The spine-tailed swift of India, for example, has been timed at over 200 miles per hour (320 km per hour). Flying is what these birds do best. They do not rest often. Except during periods of heavy rain, swifts fly all day long. It is estimated that during nesting season they fly as much as 560 miles (896 km) per day gathering food for their young. Swifts do all their feeding on the wing, catching insects in their wide mouths. In a nine-year life span, a swift can have logged 1,350,000 miles (2,160,000 km) — an average of 150,000 miles (240,000 km) per year. For American swifts, this includes a migratory round trip from North America to South America each year. In North America chimney swifts are found in central and eastern regions. West of the rocky mountains are vaux's swifts. Swifts nest on cliffs, in hollow trees, and in chimneys.

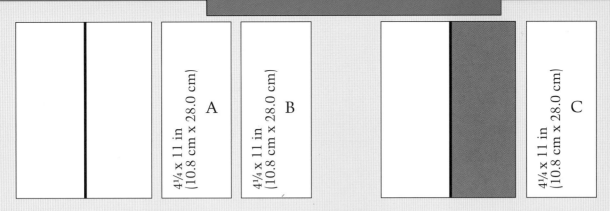

STEP 1   Measure and cut the various pieces from two sheets of bond paper.

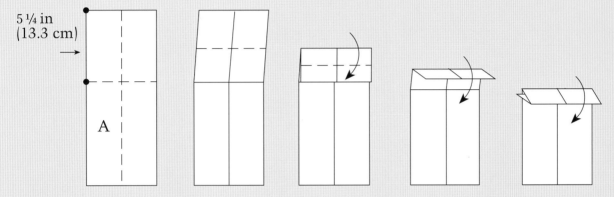

5 ¼ in
(13.3 cm)

A

STEP 2   Lay piece A flat in a vertical direction. To make the body, fold in half vertically using a valley fold. Unfold. Measure from top and valley fold, as shown. Unfold. Valley fold top portion so that top edge meets horizontal crease. Then fold top portion again so that top edge meets horizontal crease. Finally, fold over again along original horizontal crease.

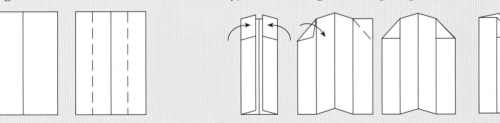

STEP 3   With upper folded part facing to the back, valley fold each side so that outer edges meet center crease, as shown. Unfold. On each side, valley fold diagonally so that top edge meets vertical crease, as shown. Then refold original vertical center crease, as shown.

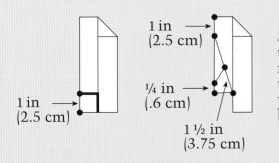

1 in
(2.5 cm)

1 in
(2.5 cm)

¼ in
(.6 cm)

1 ½ in
(3.75 cm)

STEP 4   On the left edge, measure from bottom and cut out to the center crease, as shown by heavy line. On the left edge measure from top and mark. Draw diagonal line from mark to bottom of center crease. Measure along drawn line from the bottom and mark. On the left edge, measure from bottom and mark. Join the two marks, as shown.

In the Step 1 diagram, pieces A, B, and C are each labeled:
4¼ x 11 in
(10.8 cm x 28.0 cm)

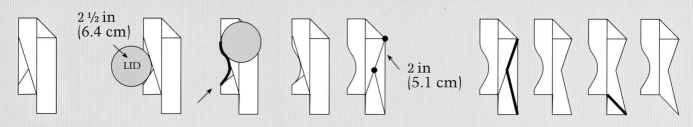

2 ½ in
(6.4 cm)

LID

2 in
(5.1 cm)

STEP 5   Using the drawn lines as an alignment guide, trace around a jar lid and cut out, as shown by heavy line.

STEP 6   From right-hand corner of diagonal fold, draw a diagonal line to the bottom center crease. From upper point, measure along diagonal line and mark. Draw diagonal line from the mark to the bottom right-hand corner. Cut out, as shown by heavy line. Then cut bottom corner diagonally, as shown.

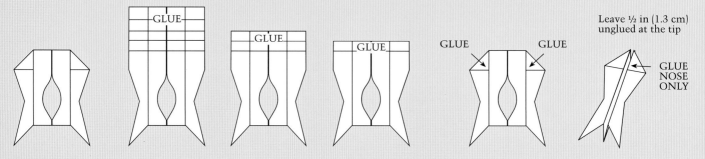

GLUE

GLUE

GLUE

GLUE   GLUE

Leave ½ in (1.3 cm) unglued at the tip

GLUE NOSE ONLY

STEP 7   Unfold body completely. Refold applying glue to all contacting surfaces, as shown. Shape body as shown. Glue nose only, leaving the tip unglued.

B

STEP 8   Lay piece B horizontally to make the wings. Fold in half vertically, using a mountain fold. Unfold. Fold in half horizontally, using a valley fold. Unfold. Then valley fold so that top edge meets horizontal crease. Fold again so that the new top edge meets the horizontal crease. Refold original horizontal crease.

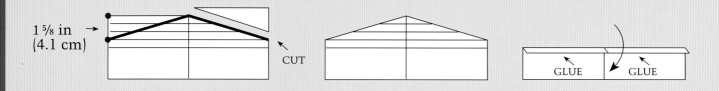

1 ⅝ in
(4.1 cm)

CUT

GLUE   GLUE

STEP 9   Unfold completely. On each side, measure and cut diagonally, as shown. Refold. Apply glue before refolding original horizontal center crease only. The folded over part is the bottom of the front edge of the wings.

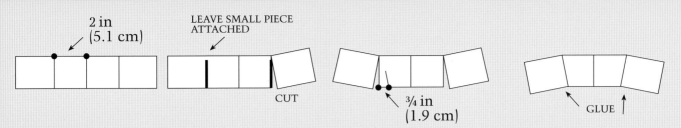

2 in
(5.1 cm)

LEAVE SMALL PIECE
ATTACHED

CUT

¾ in
(1.9 cm)

GLUE

STEP 10 To shape the wings, measure on each side, mark, and draw lines, as shown. Then, on each side, cut from the back edge as shown by heavy lines, leaving a small piece attached at the front edge. From each cut, measure and make a mark on the back edge, as shown. Align outer pieces to the marks. Glue.

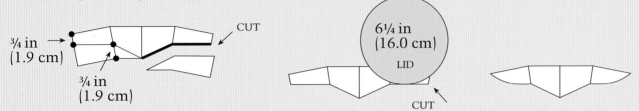

¾ in
(1.9 cm)

¾ in
(1.9 cm)

CUT

6¼ in
(16.0 cm)

LID

CUT

STEP 11 On each side, measure from the back edge along the glued line and the outer edge, make marks. Then draw lines connecting the marks, as shown. Cut along lines. Trace around a large lid and cut out to round the wingtips.

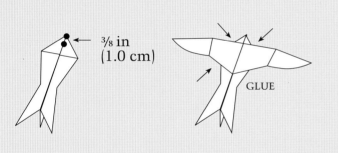

⅜ in
(1.0 cm)

GLUE

C

1¼ in x 1¾ in
(3.2 cm x 4.5 cm)

NOTE: FOR CORRECT BALANCE, MORE OR FEWER LAYERS MAY BE NEEDED DEPENDING ON THE TYPE OF PAPER AND THE AMOUNT OF GLUE USED

81

STEP 12 Measure from front of body and mark for wing position. Glue wings in place, as shown.

STEP 13 Using sheet C, measure and cut twelve small pieces, as shown. On two of the pieces, make a tracing of each side of the falcon's head shown on p 82.

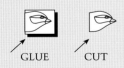

GLUE   CUT

STEP 14 Glue the pieces one on top of the other, having the tracings on the two outer sides, making sure that they are aligned. Then cut out the shape of the head, as shown.

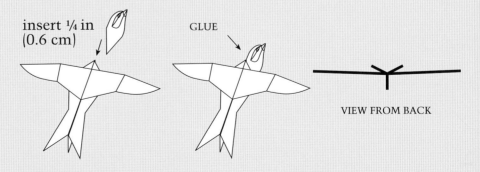

insert ¼ in
(0.6 cm)

GLUE

VIEW FROM BACK

STEP 15 Applying glue, insert the head into the front of the body. Then adjust the dihedral (upward slant of wings), as shown.

Vaux's Swift

This paper swift is about actual size. The swift is about 5 inches (12.8 cm) in length, with a wingspan of 12 in (30 cm) when fully extended. The coloration of the plumage of both male and female is similar. The back and tail are dark greenish gray. The body is lighter, with the throat being the lightest. The head is capped in black. The bill is dark gray.

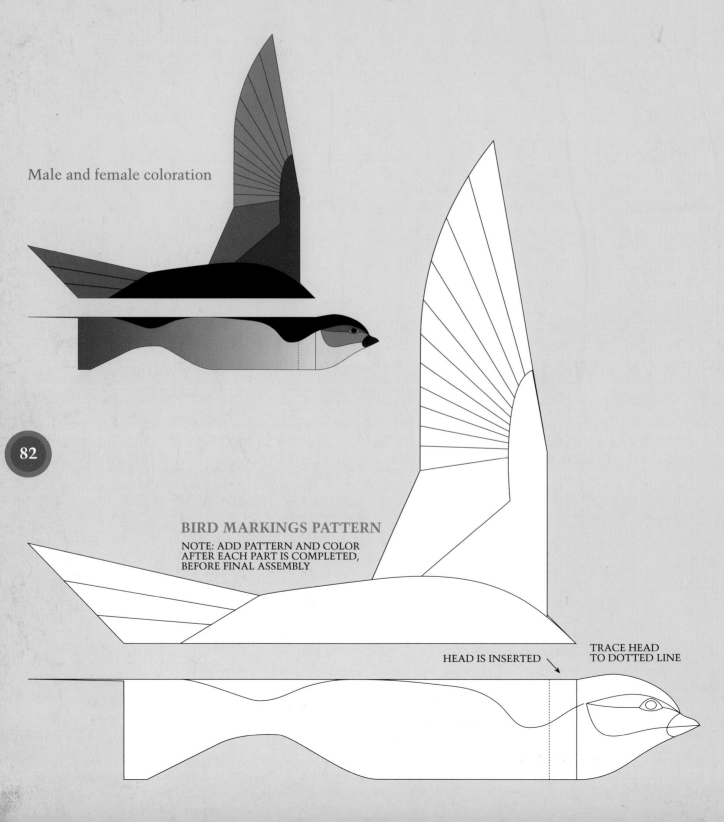

Male and female coloration

82

BIRD MARKINGS PATTERN

NOTE: ADD PATTERN AND COLOR
AFTER EACH PART IS COMPLETED,
BEFORE FINAL ASSEMBLY

HEAD IS INSERTED

TRACE HEAD
TO DOTTED LINE

Wandering Albatross

The wandering albatross spends all of its life out over the water hunting for food, except for short periods of time each year for breeding, which is spent on the cliffs of small islands out in the ocean. Albatrosses remain airborne all the time, alighting on the water briefly to eat and rest. It is thought that they even sleep on the wing. They live in the widest expanses of water on earth, the southern oceans that circle the globe uninterrupted by any large land masses, where the trade winds blow steadily out of the west. Here they are engaged in a kind of flight known as dynamic soaring, believed to be unique to albatrosses.

Albatrosses are the best of the soaring birds. They are big birds, weighing up to 20 pounds (9 kg). Their knife-like bills are up to 10 inches (25 cm) long. Their wings are especially well suited to gliding flight, having a span of up to 12 feet (3.6 meters), yet being only some 12 inches (30 cm) from front to back. The outer sections are small compared to the rest of the wing. The inner sections have five times as many feathers as most other birds. Such long, slender wings produce a large amount of lifting force with a very small amount of corresponding drag. Albatrosses seldom utilize flapping flight, only for takeoff if the wind happens to be weak. Usually they merely face into the wind, spread their wings, and the bobbing of the waves gets them airborne. On land, they face into the wind and take off from the edge of a cliff.

Dynamic soaring can be accomplished only by utilizing the wind gradient that occurs near the earth's surface. Wind always blows with a higher velocity the higher it is above the surface. Friction from the ground or water has a slowing effect on air that passes over them. For example, the wind may be blowing steadily at 40 miles per hour (64 kph) at an altitude of 50 feet (15 m). At 25 feet (7.5 m) it may be only 35 miles per hour (56 kph), at 10 feet (3 m) it may be only 30 mph (48 kph), and just over the surface only 25 mph (40 kph). This gradually decreasing wind-strength from a high level down to the surface is known as the wind gradient. Albatrosses use this, combined with the force of gravity, as a source of energy.

Beginning from about 50 feet (15 m), the albatross turns downwind, partly folding its wings. This puts it into a dive. Its speed at this point may be 30 miles per hour (48 kph). Together with the 40 mile-per-hour tail wind, its speed over the water is 70. As it descends downwind through the wind gradient, gravity increases its speed. As it descends and the windspeed decreases, which decreases drag, the relative effect of the force of gravity increases, giving the bird added acceleration, so that by the time it reaches the surface it may be traveling at over 80 miles per hour (128 kph). The albatross levels out only after descending right down into the lowest point of the trough of the swelling sea, maximizing the accelerating force, and then enters a steep climbing turn into the wind, attaining a higher altitude than from which it began and with greater speed. With this added speed it enters gliding flight. Its very efficient high-lift and low-drag wings allow it to glide a long way until it again reaches the altitude from which it began. Then it repeats the cycle. This is dynamic soaring.

CONSTRUCTING THE ALBATROSS

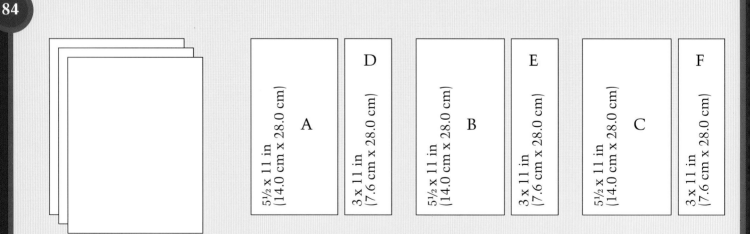

STEP 1   Using three sheets of bond paper, measure and cut the various pieces needed, as shown.

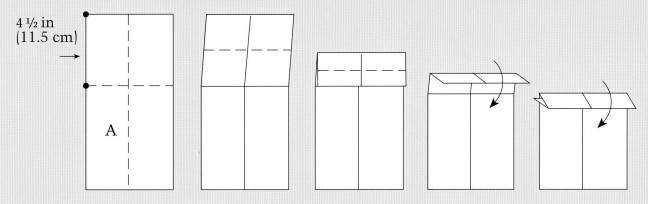

4 ½ in (11.5 cm) →

A

STEP 2 Lay piece A flat in a vertical direction. To make the body, fold in half vertically using a valley fold. Unfold. Measure from top and valley fold, as shown. Unfold. Valley fold top portion so that top edge meets horizontal crease. Then fold top portion again so that top edge meets horizontal crease. Finally, fold over again along original horizontal crease.

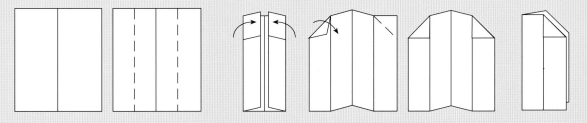

STEP 3 With upper folded part facing to the back, valley fold each side so that outer edges meet center crease, as shown. Unfold. On each side, valley fold diagonally so that top edge meets vertical crease, as shown. Then refold original vertical center crease, as shown.

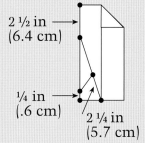

2 ½ in (6.4 cm) →

¼ in (.6 cm) →

2 ¼ in (5.7 cm)

STEP 4 On the left edge, measure from top and draw diagonal line to bottom center crease. Measure along drawn line from the bottom and mark. On the left edge, measure from bottom and mark. Join the two marks, as shown.

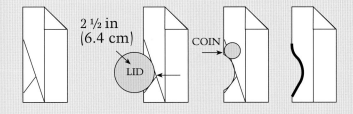

2 ½ in (6.4 cm)

LID

COIN

STEP 5 Using the drawn lines as an alignment guide, trace around a jar lid and a coin to cut rounded corners, as shown by heavy line.

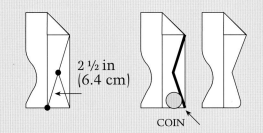

2 ½ in (6.4 cm)

COIN

STEP 6 From right-hand corner of diagonal fold, draw a diagonal line to the bottom of center crease. From the bottom, measure along diagonal line and mark. Draw diagonal line from the mark to the bottom right-hand corner. Then cut out, as shown by heavy line. To round the tail, trace around a coin.

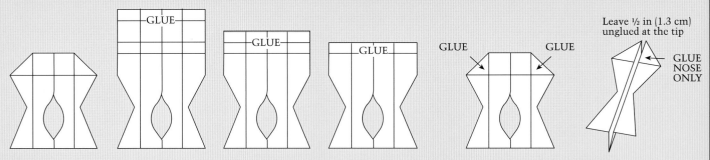

STEP 7   Unfold body completely. Refold applying glue to all contacting surfaces, as shown. Shape body as shown. Glue nose only, leaving the tip unglued.

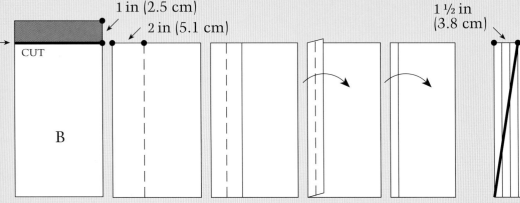

STEP 8   Lay piece B vertically to make the LEFT wing. Measure and fold vertically, using a valley fold. Unfold. Then valley fold so that left edge meets vertical crease. Fold again so that the new left edge meets the vertical crease. Refold original vertical crease.

STEP 9   Unfold completely. Measure from upper left corner and mark. Cut from mark to lower left corner, as shown.

STEP 10   Refold. Apply glue before refolding original vertical crease only. The folded over part is the front edge of the left wing. Then measure from bottom, as shown, and draw scoreline. This part becomes a tab for fastening the left- and right-hand wings together.

STEP 11   With the folded over part on the right-hand side facing to the back, measure from the bottom along the right edge and draw line. Then cut from left edge as shown by heavy line, leaving a small piece attached at the right edge. On the left edge, measure from the cut and mark, as shown. Align upper piece to the mark. Glue.

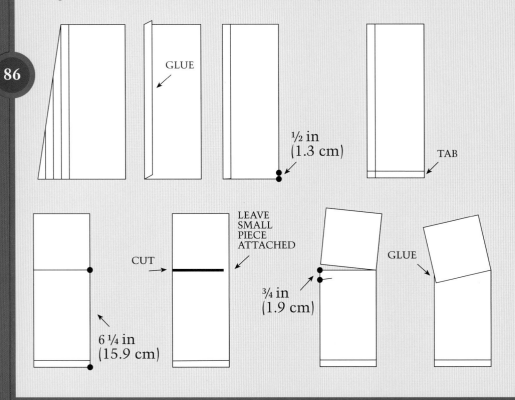

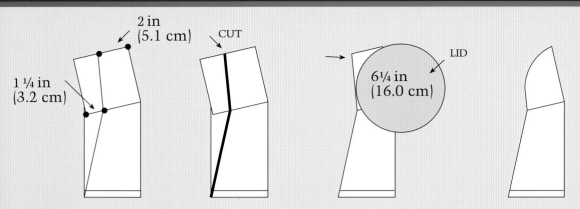

STEP 12   Measure, mark, and draw lines joining the marks, as shown. Then cut out, as shown by heavy line. Trace around a large lid and cut out to round the wingtips.

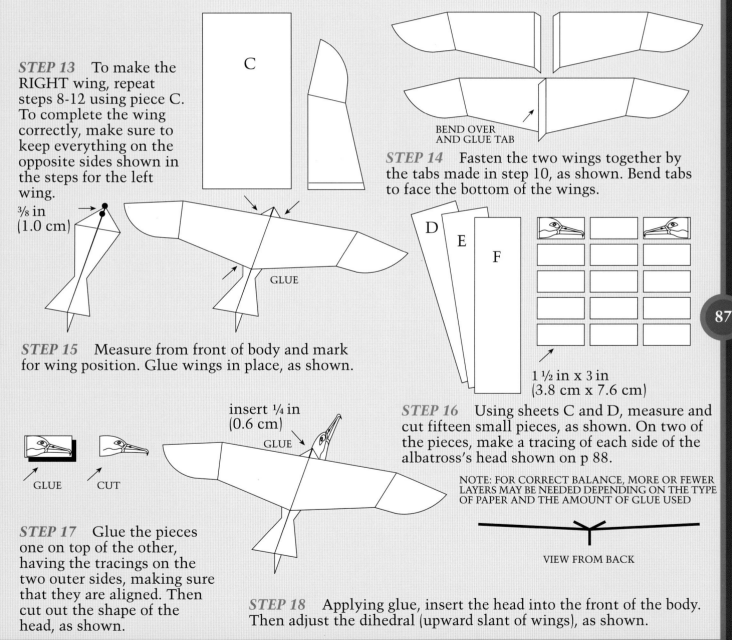

STEP 13   To make the RIGHT wing, repeat steps 8-12 using piece C. To complete the wing correctly, make sure to keep everything on the opposite sides shown in the steps for the left wing.

STEP 14   Fasten the two wings together by the tabs made in step 10, as shown. Bend tabs to face the bottom of the wings.

STEP 15   Measure from front of body and mark for wing position. Glue wings in place, as shown.

STEP 16   Using sheets C and D, measure and cut fifteen small pieces, as shown. On two of the pieces, make a tracing of each side of the albatross's head shown on p 88.

NOTE: FOR CORRECT BALANCE, MORE OR FEWER LAYERS MAY BE NEEDED DEPENDING ON THE TYPE OF PAPER AND THE AMOUNT OF GLUE USED

STEP 17   Glue the pieces one on top of the other, having the tracings on the two outer sides, making sure that they are aligned. Then cut out the shape of the head, as shown.

STEP 18   Applying glue, insert the head into the front of the body. Then adjust the dihedral (upward slant of wings), as shown.

Wandering Albatross

This paper albatross is smaller than actual size. The actual albatross is about 30 inches (75 cm) in length, with a wingspan of 144 in (360 cm) when fully extended. The coloration of both male and female is similar. They are almost entirely white. Only the primary feathers show black at the tips. The long hooked bill is yellowish. It can be up to 10 inches long (25 cm) and is razor sharp.

Male and female coloration

TRACE HEAD
TO DOTTED LINE

HEAD IS
INSERTE

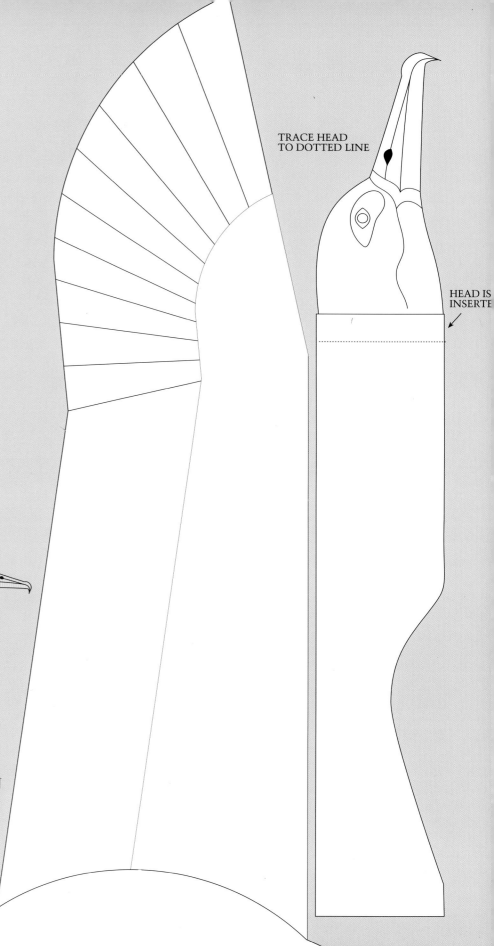

BIRD MARKINGS PATTERN

NOTE: ADD PATTERN AND COLOR
AFTER EACH PART IS COMPLETED,
BEFORE FINAL ASSEMBLY

Pterosaur

Pterosaurs were ancient flying predecessors to the birds that fill the skies today. But they were different than the birds we know. Pterosaurs were reptiles. They lived in the age of dinosaurs, their earth-bound reptile cousins. And like the dinosaurs, they are extinct. What all reptiles have in common is a body temperature that matches the air temperature, or is only slightly higher. For example, on a bright sunny day radiation from the sun provides extra warming.

Many ancient reptiles such as dinosaurs were giants by today's standards. And the pterosaurs were no exception. While some were small, about the size of a robin or blue jay, many others were the size of the present day wandering albatross. But some were enormous. The largest skeleton found so far belonged to a pterosaur that had a wingspan of 39 feet (12 m), which is the size of a small airplane, and dwarfs even the albatross.

How did these giants manage to fly? Paleontologists, who study fossils, know that they did not have wings like birds. And they had no feathers, which give bird wings their aerodynamic shape. Some had a long slender tail. Others were tailless.

Paleontologists believe that the wings of pterosaurs were made of a thin but tough leathery membrane, much like bat's wings. But because of their large size, such wings would flop about hopelessly, unless they had some kind of support, like the ribs in airplane wings or the bat's boney fingers. Some paleontologists think that ribs of some kind did exist, although no clear evidence has been found. Without ribs, the membrane would have had to be drawn taut by the pterosaur's arms and legs. In the giant creatures this would not have been practical. The lack of ribs found in the skeleton fossils is probably because they were made of cartilage instead of bone, and therefore did not fossilize. Such cartilage ribs would have given the wings the necessary stiffness and aerodynamic shape. The wing membranes were attached to both the fore and hind legs of the creature, like a bat's.

It is not known exactly how the tailless ones achieved arodynamic balance and control. Perhaps they were not very good flyers. Maybe they were capable only of short gliding hops. Some of the pterosaurs had large boney crests on their heads. By turning the head, crests may have been used as a rudder for steering.

In flight pterosaurs probably behaved much like birds. The slender shapes of many of the skeletons, with long narrow wings, suggest that some of the pterosaurs were capable of both gliding and flapping flight, and perhaps flew somewhat like sea gulls. The larger ones would have glided more than they flapped, just as large birds do, or perhaps they only glided. They may even have been able to soar.

What did pterosaurs feed on? Paleontologists think that, like birds, they fed on a wide range of things. Many of the smaller ones may have lived on insects and small creatures and plants, while some of the larger ones were probably predators like today's falcons, catching other pterosaurs. Some may have lived on fish and other marine life. However, because of their large wings, it is thought that they were not divers.

CONSTRUCTING THE PTEROSAUR

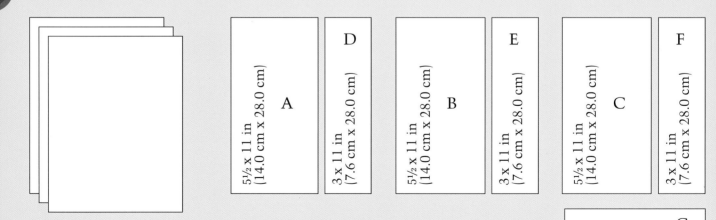

STEP 1 Using three sheets of bond paper, measure and cut the various pieces needed. One additional piece is required, as shown.

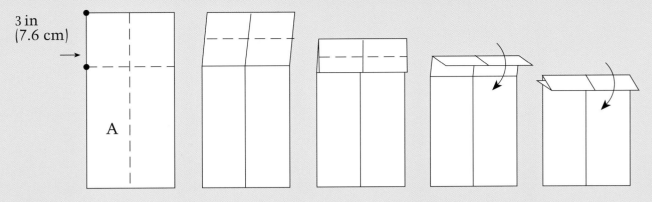

STEP 2 Lay piece A flat in a vertical direction. To make the body, fold in half vertically using a valley fold. Unfold. Measure from top and valley fold, as shown. Unfold. Valley fold top portion so that top edge meets horizontal crease. Then fold top portion again so that top edge meets horizontal crease. Finally, fold over again along original horizontal crease.

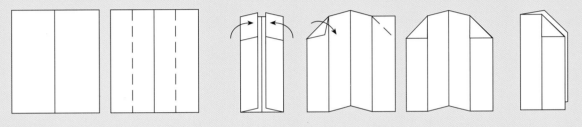

STEP 3 With upper folded part facing to the back, valley fold each side so that outer edges meet center crease, as shown. Unfold. On each side, valley fold diagonally so that top edge meets vertical crease, as shown. Then refold original vertical center crease, as shown.

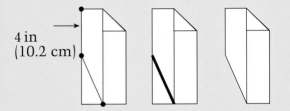

STEP 4 On the left edge, measure from top and make a mark. Cut diagonally from the mark to the bottom of the center crease, as shown by the heavy line.

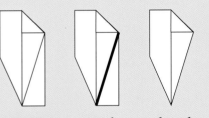

STEP 5 From the rigt-hand corner of diagonal fold, cut diagonally to the bottom of center crease, as shown by heavy line.

91

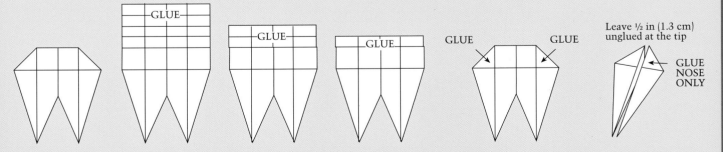

STEP 6 Unfold body completely. Refold applying glue to all contacting surfaces, as shown. Shape body as shown. Glue nose only, leaving the tip unglued.

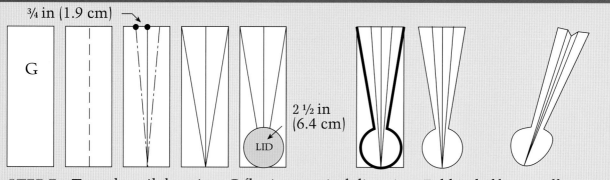

G

2 ½ in (6.4 cm)

LID

STEP 7   To make tail, lay piece G flat in a vertical direction. Fold in half vertically, using a valley fold. Unfold. On each side, measure along top edge and mark. From mark, mountain fold diagonally, as shown. Unfold. Draw diagonal line from top corner to bottom of center crease. Trace around a jar lid to shape the tail. Then cut out, as shown by heavy line. Refold to shape the tail, as shown.

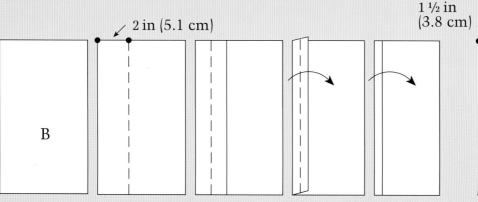

2 in (5.1 cm)

B

1 ½ in (3.8 cm)

CUT

STEP 8   Lay piece B vertically to make the LEFT wing. Measure and fold vertically, using a valley fold. Unfold. Then valley fold so that left edge meets vertical crease. Fold again so that the new left edge meets the vertical crease. Refold original vertical crease.

STEP 9   Unfold completely. Measure from upper left corner and mark. Cut from mark to lower left corner, as shown.

92

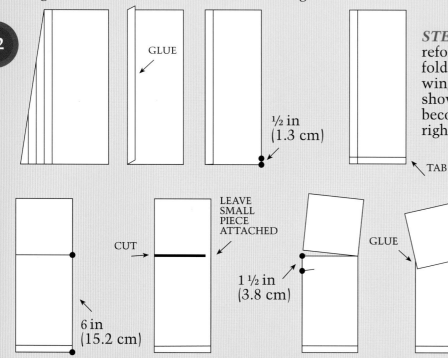

GLUE

½ in (1.3 cm)

TAB

STEP 10   Refold. Apply glue before refolding original vertical crease only. The folded over part is the front edge of the left wing. Then measure from bottom, as shown, and draw scoreline. This part becomes a tab for fastening the left- and right-hand wings together.

STEP 11   With the folded over part on the right-hand side facing to the back, measure from the bottom along the right edge and draw line. Then cut from left edge as shown by heavy line, leaving a small piece attached at the right edge. On the left edge, measure from the cut and mark, as shown. Align upper piece to the mark. Glue.

CUT

LEAVE SMALL PIECE ATTACHED

1 ½ in (3.8 cm)

GLUE

6 in (15.2 cm)

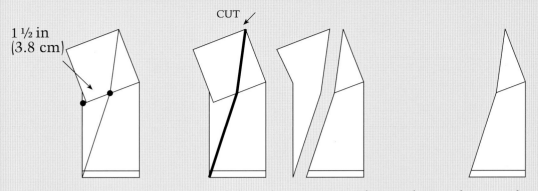

STEP 12   Measure, mark, and draw lines joining the marks, as shown. Then cut out, as shown by heavy line.

STEP 13   To make the RIGHT wing, repeat steps 8-12 using piece C. To complete the wing correctly, make sure to keep everything on the opposite sides shown in the steps for the left wing.

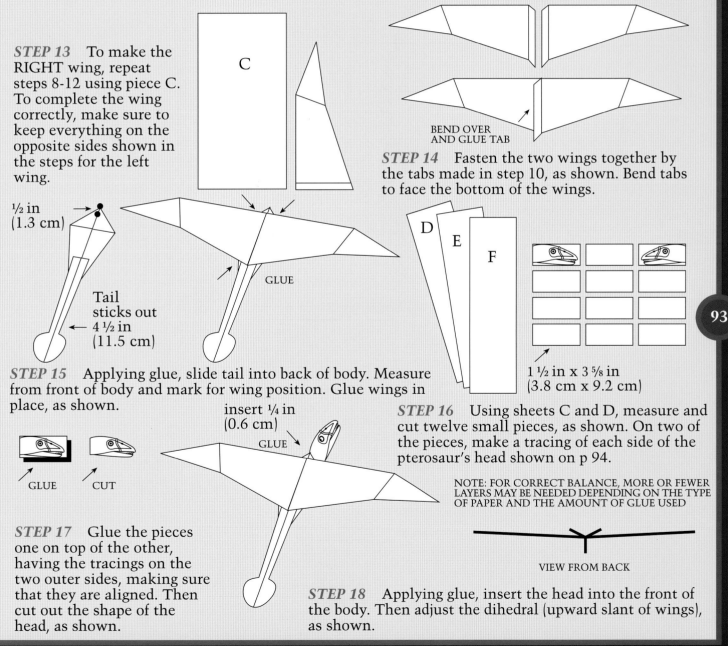

STEP 14   Fasten the two wings together by the tabs made in step 10, as shown. Bend tabs to face the bottom of the wings.

½ in (1.3 cm)

Tail sticks out ← 4 ½ in (11.5 cm)

STEP 15   Applying glue, slide tail into back of body. Measure from front of body and mark for wing position. Glue wings in place, as shown.

1 ½ in x 3 ⅝ in (3.8 cm x 9.2 cm)

STEP 16   Using sheets C and D, measure and cut twelve small pieces, as shown. On two of the pieces, make a tracing of each side of the pterosaur's head shown on p 94.

NOTE: FOR CORRECT BALANCE, MORE OR FEWER LAYERS MAY BE NEEDED DEPENDING ON THE TYPE OF PAPER AND THE AMOUNT OF GLUE USED

insert ¼ in (0.6 cm)

GLUE

VIEW FROM BACK

STEP 17   Glue the pieces one on top of the other, having the tracings on the two outer sides, making sure that they are aligned. Then cut out the shape of the head, as shown.

STEP 18   Applying glue, insert the head into the front of the body. Then adjust the dihedral (upward slant of wings), as shown.

93

Pterosaur

This paper pterosaur is smaller than the actual size of most of the prehistoric creatures, although the smallest of them were smaller. Some pterosaurs grew to be 15 feet (4.6 m) in length, with a wingspan of 39 feet (12 m) when fully extended. Nobody knows what colors they were. Use your imagination for color schemes. Some pterosaurs had large crests on their heads. Add a crest if you wish.

TRACE HEAD
TO DOTTED LINE

ALTERNATE
CRESTED
HEAD

HEAD IS
INSERTED

Male and female coloration

94

Alternate crested head

BIRD MARKINGS PATTERN

NOTE: ADD PATTERN AND COLOR
AFTER EACH PART IS COMPLETED,
BEFORE FINAL ASSEMBLY

Glossary of terms

Aerodynamics The study of the behavior of air as it flows around solid objects.

Alula feathers Small feathers found at the wrist of a bird's wing, used to provide extra lift during slow flight.

Angle of attack The upward slant, from back to front, of a wing.

Center of gravity That point on an object where it balances. The point where wings must be attached for flight.

Dihedral angle Upward slanting of wings away from the fuselage. (Downward slanting is called anhedral.)

Drag The resistance of air on moving objects, slowing them down.

Gravity The force of the earth that pulls everything downward and gives things weight.

Lift The force of air pressure beneath the wings buoying up an airplane.

Maneuver Skilfully flying in a desired direction — turn, climb, dive, stall, spin, or loop.

Molting The periodic loss of a bird's feathers and their replacement by the growth of new ones.

Ornithology The study of birds.

Primary feathers The large feathers found in the outer section of a bird's wing.

Secondary feathers The feathers found nearest the body along the back edge of a bird's wing.

Soaring Gliding flight where the upward motion provided by warmed air is greater than the rate at which gravity pulls a bird downward.

Thermal A column of rising air warmed by radiation from the sun's rays heating the ground.

Thrust The force, provided either by gravity or wing flapping, that moves a bird forward through the air.

Trim Making small adjustments to the wings and tail to affect the flight of a bird.

Wing loading The amount of weight a given area of wing is required to lift.

Quill The hollow flexible shaft of a feather.

Further reading

Jack Anthony. *Feathered Wings: A Study of the Flight of Birds.* Methuen and Co., London, 1953.

John Bull and John Farrand, Jr. *The Audubon Society Field Guide to North American Birds.* Alfred A. Knopf, New York, 1977.

Chandler S. Robbins, Bertel Bruun, and Herbert S. Zim. *Birds of North America.* Golden Press, New York, 1966.

R.T. Peterson. *A Field Guide to the Birds.* Houghton Mifflin, Boston, 1980.

Georg Rüppell. *Bird Flight.* Van Nostrand Reinhold, New York, 1977.

Norman Schmidt. *Discover Aerodynamics with Paper Airplanes.* Peguis, Winnipeg, 1991.

J.C. Welty. *The Life of Birds.* W.B. Saunders, Philadelphia, 1975.

John K. Terres. *Flashing Wings.* Doubleday & Co., Garden City, 1968.

Index